Religion, spirituality and older people

Kenneth Howse

Centre for Policy on Ageing

First published in 1999
by the Centre for Policy on Ageing
25-31 Ironmonger Row
London EC1V 3QP
Tel: +44 020 7253 1787
Fax: +44 020 7490 4206
Email: cpa@cpa.org.uk
www.cpa.org.uk

© 1999 Centre for Policy on Ageing

British Library Cataloguing in Publication Data
A catalogue record for this book is available from the British Library

ISBN 090413993X

To obtain a CPA Publications Catalogue and details of other CPA Reports please contact the Publications Officer, Centre for Policy on Ageing, 25-31 Ironmonger Row, London EC1V 3QP.

Printed by Redwood Books, Kennet Way, Trowbridge, Wiltshire BA14 8RN
Cover design by Jeremy Austen

FOREWORD

Within our culture there remains an expectation that ageing heightens the life of the spirit. We look to older people for re-affirmation of values, and a coherent perspective on ultimate goals. In the past religious and spiritual beliefs have typically provided that coherence for the greater part of the older population. Yet there has been relatively little investigation carried out in Britain into the spiritual beliefs and practices of older people. By contrast, in the United States research into religion, spirituality and ageing is well established, regularly represented in the annual meetings of the Gerontological Society of America. In part this reflects the greater participation by Americans in churches and other religious organisations. In Britain church attendance has steadily declined. However there is good reason to think that spiritual beliefs are held by the greater part of the British older population and find expression in a wide variety of ways. They contribute significantly to people's perceived quality of life, and help them cope with the losses and crises of ageing. Practical and policy questions arise about sustaining and developing beliefs, whether spiritual or philosophical, that enhance life in the face of death. These questions have more salience in our country nowadays precisely because participation rates in religious institutions are relatively low.

I greatly welcome this report from the Centre for Policy on Ageing. It is a good illustration of CPA's commitment to identifying and exploring new areas for policy analysis. It represents a long period of reflection on CPA's part about the kind of report that is required in this particular field. It takes account of the variety of spiritual forms of life present in Britain today. The life of the established Christian churches, although very important, can no longer be assumed to provide the principal framework for inquiry in a society that is both ethnically diverse and secularised. Although it gives due weight to US research findings it makes clear that we cannot rely on them as a guide to practice in Britain. We need to undertake our own investigations, and as the author of this report stresses, our own debate about the wider significance of religious and spiritual language to well-being in later life. But at the same time the report illustrates the potential importance of this field of inquiry for enhancing quality of life. Kenneth Howse has done an excellent job not only in integrating a large collection of disparate material, but also in elucidating key questions for further inquiry and discussion.

Peter G. Coleman
Professor of Psychogerontology, University of Southampton

iii

CONTENTS

INTRODUCTION

In 1961 a report on religion and older people was included in the first of the United States White House Conferences on Aging. Policy makers and academic gerontologists lent a willing ear to religious leaders who thought that they had an important contribution to make to the improvement of the well-being of older people in the USA. The conference marked an awakening of research interest into the precise nature of that contribution, and now, nearly forty years later, religion has an established place on the research agenda of gerontologists and policy makers in the USA. Indeed the research literature bulks so large that religious gerontology has become a separate specialism with its own learned journal.

In Britain, where the policy problems and challenges facing health and social services drive so much of the research into the position of older people, it has taken somewhat longer for the topic of religion to receive the kind of attention that is devoted to it in the USA. Over the last few years, however, there has been a clearly perceptible quickening of interest in the topic on this side of the Atlantic. Much of this interest, as in the USA, comes from the churches and other religious organisations as they ask themselves about their roles and responsibilities in the changing circumstances of what is now familiarly known as an ageing society. Interest, however, is by no means confined to those who occupy a religious standpoint. As the churches in Britain have started to take a fresh look at the position of older people in society, social researchers have started to investigate issues like provision for the spiritual needs of older people. No clearer evidence of this quickening of interest is needed than the prominence given to the theme of spirituality in the 1999 annual conference of the British Society of Gerontology. The purpose of this CPA report is to set these emerging investigations and inquiries in their wider context and examine some of the issues that arise from them.

Twenty years ago Paul Gaine (1978), a Roman Catholic priest working in England, complained of the absence of any discussion of ageing in books on pastoral theology and pastoral counselling and a similar absence of discussion about the role of the churches in "technical treatises on ageing". In the USA cornucopia seems to have taken the place of dearth. The situation in the United Kingdom could hardly be so described, despite the recent publication of a report from the charity Counsel and Care about the spiritual dimension of care in residential homes (Regan and Smith 1997), an anthology of articles on spirituality

1

and ageing (Jewell 1998), a review by Davie and Vincent (1998) and training materials for the clergy from the Methodist Homes Association and the Christian Council on Ageing (1998). Gaine perhaps would find less cause for complaint now than formerly, though there is still relatively little theological discussion of ageing published on this side of the Atlantic. And for those whose professional concern with older people has a secular base, whether as researchers or as providers of care, not *that* much has changed since the late 1970s, though undoubtedly there is a growing interest among service providers and academics in the uses and benefits of what is usually called spiritual care (Neuberger 1997; Cobb and Robshaw 1998).

It is this sparseness of British writing on the connections between religion and ageing that forces us to look to the American literature to consider how the topic has been explored by different professions and academic disciplines. For there can be no doubt that the literature on the connection between religion and ageing is very disparate. Different professions (such as medicine, nursing and social work) and academic disciplines (such as epidemiology and social psychology) ask different questions and rest their inquiries on different foundations. In this respect the topic of religion and ageing reflects much of what is written about ageing and older people. Here, however, complexity is further complicated by the presence of contributions from a profession (minister of religion) and an academic discipline (theology) which have for their foundations the ideas and beliefs of particular religious traditions. They ask questions and develop ideas from within an avowedly religious viewpoint, which is usually, though not always, that of Christianity or Judaism.

It is not the purpose of the present report to review even in a summary way *all* the different branches of the American literature on the connection between religion and ageing. Much of this work (reports of research as well as more discursive pieces) is firmly embedded in the context of American society. It documents the religious beliefs and practices of older Americans or discusses the role of American churches and other religious organisations in an ageing society. What this study seeks to do is to gather together equivalent material for the United Kingdom. The first two chapters of this report transpose to a British setting a theme which has been developed largely in an American context. They fill in some of the factual and historical background to the discussion of policy issues which follows. They also serve to document, firstly, the interest shown by British social researchers in the religious life of older people in this country and, secondly, the interest shown by the churches and other religious organisations in this country in the well-being of older people

A great deal is known about the place of religion in the lives of older Americans. For American social researchers who wanted to describe and understand the lives of older Americans, religion was a phenomenon they could hardly ignore. There was (and is), quite simply, 'a lot of it about'. To what extent can the same be said of older people in Britain? Although British social researchers have paid much less attention to the place of religion in the lives of older people in Britain than their American counterparts, there is still enough to be able, for example, to make some comparisons between Britain and the USA. We can ask how commonly religious commitment is to be found among older people in Britain, whether it has declined in recent years, and whether it is more common in older than in younger age groups. Chapter 1 looks at survey data from the 1940s to the present day to see what light they shed on these questions.

Chapter 2 looks at the view that churches and other religious organisations in the UK take of their responsibilities towards older people in an ageing society. A church or other religious organisation which speaks out on ageing and the position of older people may engage with matters of *public* policy by addressing itself to the rights and wrongs of current social practice or government policy. The focus of this chapter, however, is the policy and practice of the churches themselves. What have they said about the nature of their contribution to the well-being of older people? How have they sought to formulate their own institutional responsibilities to older people as well as the responsibilities of individuals of all ages who constitute their membership?

In some respects both these chapters stand alone. Each could be read without serious loss of intelligibility apart from the rest of the report. They are not so much essential steps in an argument which culminates in the discussion of the final chapter as reviews of two quite distinct bodies of literature. On the one hand, there are questions of fact and theory that may be interesting to students of the social or behavioural sciences (for example, are older people really more religious than younger people or is this just a myth?) but are perhaps of uncertain relevance to the development of social policy for an ageing society; and on the other hand, there are policy issues and debates which are clearly of interest to churches and other religious organisations (since they concern their own policies and practices) but may have little resonance for discussions of *public* policy on ageing. Both these two chapters make it clear therefore that it is possible to explore the connection between religion and ageing without raising questions about public policy.

What makes this material of interest from the point of view of public policy is the possibility of a connection between religion and *successful* ageing. And Chapter

3 examines this connection – the claim that religion has a positive contribution to make to well-being in later life – from the point of view of public policy. What, if any, are the implications of this connection for the development of social policy in an ageing society? This broad issue will be considered in the light of three more specific questions. What are the practical implications of the (American) research findings on the association between religion and well-being in later life? Should service providers and policy makers, as well as researchers, expand their conception of individual well-being in later life to include a spiritual dimension? Is there anything in the religious standpoint which might help meet concern about the 'roleless role' of old age?

1

RELIGIOUS COMMITMENT AMONG OLDER PEOPLE IN BRITAIN

INTRODUCTION

In 1947 the pioneering social research organisation Mass Observation published a report entitled *Puzzled people*. Based on a questionnaire survey of a random sample of 500 people in a north London suburb, it is one of the first post-war British studies of popular attitudes to religion and ethics. In common with most subsequent studies of religious belief and practice in this country, it was found that only a small minority of the respondents could be described as active and orthodox Christians, though belief in a deity and in life after death were much more common. In fact more than two-thirds of the respondents affirmed a belief in God, rather more than the proportion of those who affirmed a belief in life after death, though these too were in the majority. Private prayer and support for the churches as agencies for the moral education of children were relatively common among the 'non-active' believers in the sample (and not all that uncommon even among the non-believers, one quarter of whom said that they prayed on occasions to a God whose existence they doubted). How should the position of those individuals who were neither active Christians nor avowed non-believers be understood? Were they people who combined marked religious leanings with disaffection from the mainstream churches? It seems not. The prevalent attitude was one of goodwill towards the idea of religion and religious faith, showing a benevolent neutrality rather than hostility or commitment. A very similar attitude of negligible commitment coupled with minimal acceptance of prevailing beliefs and social habits was found to be common among the 200 people interviewed by Seebohm Rowntree and George Lavers (1951) for their early post-war study of 'English life and leisure'.

Much of the empirical investigation of religious belief and practice by social researchers in post-war Britain has followed the lines laid down by *Puzzled people*. It has sought both to understand and to gauge the nature and extent of popular support for, or adherence to, organised religion. It has tried also to document and understand the religious beliefs and practices of the majority of the population who have little to do with organised religion. What is the nature and significance of those manifestations of individual religiosity to be found outside, or on the edge of, the domain of organised religion? The investigations have been conducted mostly by sociologists who hope that the survey data will throw light on the question of the secularisation of British society. Their main interest, which is the detection, analysis and interpretation of social trends, touches upon the concerns of the gerontologist only insofar as they have asked about the demographic characteristics shared by the people whose religious beliefs and practices conform to the requirements or expectations of organised religion. It is, for the most part, to these data that the gerontologist must look in order to determine how common religious commitment is among older people in this country, and whether older people are different in this respect from younger people. Not surprisingly perhaps, there are very few UK studies which have looked in any detail at the religious concerns and practices of older people. There are, as we shall see, a few studies which have touched on religious matters in the context of a wider inquiry into the concerns and interests of older people. However, these usually have been interested mainly in the association of older people with a church as an indicator either of continuing social participation or of sources of social support outside the family.

THE DECLINE IN ORGANISED CHRISTIANITY AND THE GROWTH OF RELIGIOUS DIVERSITY

The essential background to any discussion of religion and older people in Britain is what appears to most observers as the long-term decline in the position of the Christian churches over the course of this century, a decline which has persisted in the post-war years, albeit with some fluctuations (see Martin 1967; Currie et al 1977; Gill 1993). Fewer people attend churches for normal services and the use of churches even for rites of passage has declined. Fewer people assent to, or indeed know about, the teachings of the churches (Barker et al 1992). Fewer people believe that the churches or their teachings have an important part to play either in their own lives or in the life of society as a whole (Svennegig 1988).

The pattern of uniform decline among the mainstream Christian churches is graphically illustrated by results from two national church censuses (how many people in church on a given Sunday?), the first carried out in 1979 and the second in 1989 (Brierley 1991). It is estimated that in this ten-year period there was a drop of 8% in adult church attendance, the largest fall being in the Catholic Church who saw their congregations decline by 14%. About half a million people ceased to go to church. Adult attendances have fallen off as the churches fail to recruit younger children and teenagers to fill the places left by the deaths of older churchgoers (Gill 1993). The major exception to this pattern of change during the 1980s was the growth of the independent churches (or 'House' Churches), Pentecostal churches and Afro-Caribbean churches. Brierley estimates that adult attendances in these churches grew by almost 50% during the 1980s thereby offsetting the decline in the other 'Free Protestant' churches (but not in the Christian churches as a whole). This particular phenomenon owes much to immigration from the West Indies in the same way as the robustness of the Catholic Church in the earlier post-war period owed much to immigration from Ireland (Hornsby-Smith 1987).

Evidence for declining church attendance is evidence for a decline in communal forms of religious observance prescribed by the Christian religion, and tells us about the conformity of individuals to some of the requirements of established religious institutions, and hence also about the authority possessed by these institutions. It is evident, however, that a religious outlook, even perhaps a specifically Christian outlook, may flourish outside the body of active churchgoers, and in spite of the waning authority of the churches. It is an important part of the Christian tradition that there is more to true religion than conformity to prescribed ritual observances and creeds. It should have far-reaching ramifications for the way people live their lives, for what they feel and think and do about all aspects of their situation in life. Impatience with rigid requirements of practice and belief might perhaps cause many people to detach themselves from any kind of organised Christianity (whether mainstream churches or independent) while remaining loyal to what they see as its *essential* teachings.

There is no evidence, however, to suggest that this kind of private or domestic attachment to the Christian religion is at all widespread. On the persistence of private as opposed to public religious practices, such as private prayer and Bible reading, there is little data one way or the other (see though Gorer 1955; Forster 1995). Avowals of religious belief are undoubtedly more common than religious observance. In a Gallup poll conducted in 1963, 71% of adults claimed to believe in God (Martin 1968). Only half of these, however, believed in the personal God of the Christian religion. Similar figures were reported by the European Values Study (Abrams et al 1985). That there has been a decline in orthodox Christian belief in recent years seems clear (for example, Barker et al 1992). The evidence points therefore to increasing detachment from the patterns of practice *and* belief prescribed by the Christian churches. It seems, furthermore, that as attachment to the institutions of organised Christianity weakens, so are there fewer people willing to ascribe importance to the Christian religion for the way they live their lives (Svennegig 1988; Barker et al 1992).

The main question which arises for the sociologist of religion from this change in the position and authority of the Christian churches is its relationship with the phenomenon of secularisation. The drift away from organised Christianity appears to be a drift towards an increasingly secular outlook. Are there other possibilities to be considered before this appearance is accepted as reality?

Recent decades have seen an expansion in the proportion of the population attached to other forms of organised religion besides Christianity, most notably Islam and Hinduism as the main religions of the India subcontinent. (The exception is Judaism which has suffered the same sort of decline as Christianity, Jacobovits 1981.) In the 1997 British Social Attitudes survey, 3.7% of the population declared their allegiance to a non-Christian religion (Jowell et al 1997), which is about double the figure in the 1985 survey (Jowell et al 1985). If Britain is a more secular society than it was fifty years ago, it is also a more religiously diverse society. Ethnic diversity has increased religious diversity. One consequence of this phenomenon, especially in view of the abundant evidence for relatively high levels of religious participation among minority ethnic groups (for example, Modood and Berthoud 1996), is that the numbers of people attached to organised religion have been boosted by the numbers attached to non-Christian religions. The position of dominance held by organised Christianity has been weakened as other forms of organised religion have taken root and grown.

A change in the pattern of religious loyalties is not the same thing, however, as a brake on the process of secularisation. Non-Christian forms of organised religion may prove to be no more immune to secularisation than Christianity. Kosmin and Levy (1978) and Miller et al (1996) both present evidence to this effect for the Jewish community, where for many people religious observance appears to have been increasingly emptied of its religious significance, though it has retained its importance as a sign of belonging to the Jewish people. And Modood and Berthoud (1996) present analogous evidence for a wider range of minority ethnic groups. The longer that migrants have spent in Britain, the less likely are they to say that religion is very important to how they live their lives.

Until recently, however, sociologists of religion were interested less in the diversity of established and recognised forms of organised religion, and more in the possibility of social forms of religion which might persist or flourish apart from involvement in organised religion (Davie 1994). They interested themselves in the emergence and growth of those cults or new religious movements which constitute a kind of religious 'underground'; with the survival of what is usually called popular or folk religion (for an investigation of popular religion in Islington see Abercrombie et al 1970); and last of all with the development of what German sociologist Thomas Luckmann (1967) called a new social form of religion, namely 'invisible religion'. Whereas cults are in effect examples of 'alternative' churches (requiring commitment from their members no less than more recognised churches), popular religion and invisible religion are phenomena of a different order. They have nothing to do with institutional allegiance, and serve therefore to underline the importance of distinguishing between individual religiosity and religious commitment. Religious commitment, for the sociologist of religion, is a way of assessing the religiousness of an individual in terms of his or her participation in, or loyalty to, a religious institution or group.

Wherever popular religion and invisible religion are found, they are evidence of the persistence of an unsecularised outlook among people who have little to do with organised religion (Towler 1985). In *Puzzled people* popular religion is taken to include practices like the use of lucky charms or the casting of horoscopes or the invocation of a supernatural agency in times of crisis. It is a form of religion which stands in contrast to that of the active and orthodox believer, being something "passive and little dwelt upon – elbowed into a corner of the mind which it shares with competing beliefs of all kinds, and from where it is summoned at moments in life when habit and know-how cannot assist, and whence it returns in the light of day" (Abercrombie et al 1970). Invisible religion is something different from this, relying for its existence, not on the preservation of a shared tradition of belief and practice, but on the desire and ability of individuals to piece together their own "private systems of ultimate significance" from the assortment of religious ideas or "themes" that are on offer (Luckmann 1967). Existing apart from any specialised social institutions, it is nevertheless a potentially important manifestation of individual religiosity precisely because of the nature of the ideas which it appropriates. And unlike popular religion, which is usually accompanied by practical indifference to the central spiritual concerns of the major world religions, invisible religion often takes these concerns to heart.

It is one thing to investigate the public or private attachment of older people to organised or institutional religion. It is perhaps somewhat more difficult to investigate the persistence among them of popular religion, and more difficult still to investigate the growth of invisible religion. It is not at all easy to look for religiousness apart from individual participation in, or loyalty to, a religious institution or group. With only a few exceptions, most of the survey reports cited in this chapter are concerned with institutional religion. What is the nature and extent of older people's participation in institutional religion and how much importance do they ascribe to it? Whatever question is asked, however, it is essential that it is seen against a background of historical change.

THE SURVEYS: HOW COMMON IS CHURCHGOING IN THE OLDER POPULATION?

Religious observance is much more common in the USA than in Britain (see for example Greeley 1992). What is true of the population as a whole is also true, not surprisingly, of the older populations in the two countries. In the USA the majority (52%) of people aged 65 years or more attend religious services regularly (PRRC 1994). To find similar rates for church attendance among older people in the United Kingdom it is necessary to look outside England, and at surveys conducted some years ago. In the 1950s, in Welsh-speaking Gwynnedd, 54% of older men and 58% of older women attended chapel at least once every Sunday (Owen 1960). A more recent survey of older people (65 years or more) in Armagh in Northern Ireland also reported very high rates of churchgoing with 65% of men and 69% of women attending church at least once a fortnight (Williamson 1975). What is more, about 30% of the sample, men and women, said that they would like to go to church more often, but were prevented from doing so either by ill-health or by lack of transport. In northeast Scotland in the 1970s, 49% of Protestants and 71% of Roman Catholics attended weekly (Reid 1978) and all but 4% of the sample (65+) belonged to one or the other of these two groups. Here again, it seems likely that the figures for regular attendance underestimate the true level of attachment to the church, as 40% of the female non-attenders were housebound. (Rory William's 1990 study of the Protestant legacy in the same part of Scotland in the late 1980s shows much lower rates of weekly attendance among older Aberdonians at 15%.)

In England the picture is very different, whether we look at small local studies or large national studies. In Bethnal Green in the 1950s "most [older] people rarely, if ever, went to church" (Townsend 1957). Only 13% of this solidly working-class sample said that they went to church as much as once a month. On the other side of London, in Hammersmith, an "investigation of the social and economic circumstances of one hundred people of over seventy years of age" found that 12% of its rather small sample went to church regularly (National Co of Soc Service 1954). And in yet another part of London, Wandsworth, about thirty years later, 19% of the population aged 75 years or more "took part in religious activities" (Boyle 1987). In South Shields in 1964, 19% of the older population were regular churchgoers (Hanson 1964). Jeremy Tunstall's (1966) study of older people living alone found that 17.3% had been to church in the previous week. Less frequent attendance is more common. One in three of the elderly people in Qureshi and Walker's study (1989) of family caregivers went to church at least occasionally and half of these rated church membership as very important to them.

A more recent study in Southampton noted that 32% of a sample of older people "went to church sometimes" (Coleman 1990). And on a council housing estate in Hull, 26.5% of the older people ("61 years up") in the sample went to church at least sometimes, though few of these attended more than once a month, and "attendance at normal services [as opposed to rites of passage] was of very little importance" irrespective of age (Forster 1995). Among older people in England regular attendance at religious services is a minority activity, and although this is not revealed by the studies cited above, it is likely that the minority is more sizeable in some parts of the country than in others. Attendance at Anglican services, for example, varies considerably by diocese being much higher in rural Hereford than London or Birmingham. Another factor affecting aggregate figures for attendance at religious services in an area is the size of the local Roman Catholic population, as Roman Catholics tend to be more frequent attenders than, say, Anglicans (Gill 1993).

One of the earliest surveys to ask about religious belief and practice in a nationally representative sample is Geoffrey Gorer's 1955 exploration of English character. Twenty per cent of the people aged 65 years or more attended church at least once a week; 30% more than once a month. A few studies conducted more than thirty years later suggest that there has been some fall-off in attendance since this time, though the figures are not strictly comparable. The English arm of the European Values Study found that 17% of retired males and 40% of retired females attended church at least once a month (Abrams et al 1985). In 1987, 22.1% of retired people (14% of men and 27% of women) participating in a large health and lifestyle survey had been to a place of worship in the previous two weeks (Cox 1987). These large male–female differences are confirmed in the data from the British Social Attitudes survey (see Figure 1).

The 1989 English church census estimated that 12% of men and 14% of women aged 65 years or more were in church on 'census Sunday' (Brierley 1991). However, in surveys conducted on behalf of the Independent Broadcasting Authority (now the Independent Television Commission), higher rates of regular attendance "at a place of worship" were reported than even in Gorer's survey (Gunter and Vinery 1994). Twenty-three per cent of people aged 55 years or over said that they went to a place of worship at least weekly.

Aggregate figures for regular attendance at a place of worship conceal quite large differences between different religious groups – Christian and non-Christian. In Gunter and Vinery's study for the Independent Television Commission, weekly attendance at a place of worship was more common among older Hindus (41%) and older Muslims (69%) than among older people in the

Figure 1 Attendance of males and females 65 years+ at place of worship, 1983–97

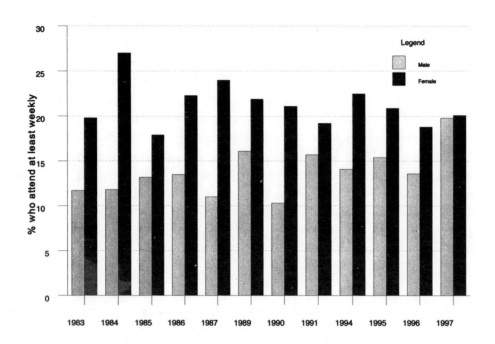

general population (see above). Among Jews, on the other hand, regular attendance at a place of worship appears to be less common than among the general population. Regular attendance at a synagogue was reported by only 14% of the older (65+) respondents in a 1970s study of the Jewish community in Redbridge (Kosmin and Levy 1978), somewhat less than the 16% estimated for the rest of outer London in the 1979 church census (National Initiative in Evangelism 1980). Perhaps the most notable feature of regular synagogue attendance (at all ages) is that the proportion of male and female attenders is almost the exact opposite of what is found in the Christian churches. Males are more likely to be regular attenders than females.

There are differences also to be found between the various Christian churches. Roman Catholics, for example, tend to be more frequent churchgoers at all ages than individuals who describe themselves as belonging to the Church of England. Two-fifths of the Catholics surveyed by Hornsby-Smith (1987) attended church at least weekly, and regular attendance was more common among older than younger Catholics. In the same way, membership of one of the Free Protestant churches also seems to be associated with relatively regular attendance, especially in the older age groups (for example Clark 1970). Weekly attendance was reported by as many as 86% of the members of Black Pentecostal churches in a recent survey (Gunter and Vinery 1994).

Some part of these differences may be explained by the peculiar position of the Church of England as the established national church with all that that entails. Caribbean-born Anglicans, for example, are much more likely to be regular churchgoers than British-born white Anglicans (Modood and Berthoud 1996). Of more general significance perhaps is the meaning which participation in collective worship may have among some minority ethnic groups. A survey of British Jewry, for example, claimed that "for most Jews, religious observance is a means of identifying with the Jewish community rather than expression of religious faith" (Miller et al 1996). And there seems little doubt that communal worship serves a similar social function among other ethnic groups, enhancing the attractions of its more strictly religious functions (Modood and Berthoud 1996).

THE SURVEYS: RELIGIOUS ORGANISATIONS AND OTHER VOLUNTARY COMMUNITY ORGANISATIONS

There is no question about the relative importance of the church among voluntary association memberships of the aged. Study after study in different parts of the nation and in different types of community have found that the aged are more apt to be church members than members of any other one type of voluntary organisation and, indeed, than of all other associations together. (Moberg 1965)

The nation in this case is the USA, not Britain. What can we say about comparable levels of formal social participation in religious organisations in the UK?

Membership of a church or religious organisation is usually taken to indicate a degree of associational commitment (Lenski 1961) greater than that attested by mere attendance at communal worship. Outside the Church of England nearly all of the Protestant churches distinguish between members and attenders or adherents; and within the Church of England there is a big difference between the occasional attender and someone who has been confirmed or is on the parish electoral roll. An even greater degree of associational commitment is shown by those people who join and participate in the wide variety of affiliated organisations, societies and committees that are usually connected with the life of the church (or mosque or synagogue) in the local community. Hornsby-Smith (1989) estimated that about one-eighth of all Catholic adults were active members of parish organisations. In churches which are run on more democratic lines as, for example, the Methodist Church (Jerrome 1989) and Black Pentecostal churches (Calley 1965; Howard 1987), the levels of active participation among adults may be much higher. Much of the burden of this kind of voluntary activity is taken up by people in the older age groups. Data from the 1997 National Survey of Volunteering (Davis Smith 1998) show that the modal age of people who had undertaken voluntary work for a religious organisation in the previous year was 55–75 years. The churches rely very heavily on the contribution of people in their Third Age.

Information on membership of religious organisations as one type of community organisation among others is fairly thin on the ground in Britain, though some idea of the importance of religious groups for formal social participation can be gained from studies of volunteering. In 1991 there were more regular formal volunteers working in and for religious groups than any other area of activity (Knapp et al 1995). And for some groups of older people, those in Abbeyfield Homes for example (Davis Smith 1995), there is little doubt that the church is the main channel for their continuing active involvement in community activities.

A few studies (for example, Cox 1987) present figures for churchgoing as one type of leisure activity among others, but this is not quite the same thing as *formal* social participation. There are one or two local studies which suggest membership of old people's clubs is, or was, more common than membership of religious organisations (Townsend 1957; Chester CC 1984), though in Wales, where Clare Wenger (1993) reports remarkably high levels of membership of religious organisations among older people, the opposite situation prevails. The best information comes from a large national survey of older people conducted in the 1970s (Hunt 1978). Thirty-eight per cent of men and 34% of women aged 65 years or more belonged to some kind of voluntary community organisation. For men as well as for women, religious organisations attracted more members than any other category of voluntary organisation, though twice as many women (15.8%) as men (7.7%) were members. For men, though not for women, there are other types of voluntary association – the British Legion, Trade Unions and organisations for OAPs – which have only slightly fewer members (5.8%) than religious organisations. Similar figures for membership of religious organisations are reported by Abrams (1980). Of the women aged 65–74 and those aged 75+, 13.3% and 16% respectively were members of a religious or church-based organisation. Membership was less common among the men – 8.4% of the 65–74 age group and 8.2% of the 75+ age group. It is only for the 75+ age group, however, that a comparison is made between church groups and other groups: the proportion of the sample belonging to clubs for the elderly is the same as that belonging to church groups.

THE SURVEYS: THE DIFFERENCES BETWEEN OLDER PEOPLE AND YOUNGER PEOPLE

The view expressed by one of the younger inhabitants of Metrop in the 1947 Mass Observation study that religion "is more for old people, isn't it?" is confirmed, in one respect and emptied of its normative content, by the results of the more considered inquiries of the investigators. "Metrop churches on a given Sunday contain predominantly women, old people, educated people." It is also confirmed, with some qualifications, by virtually every study that has subsequently been undertaken on this topic, and applies not only to participation in communal worship, but also to religious belief and most other variables that have been used to investigate religious commitment or religiosity.

Table 1 Regular attendance at a place of worship by gender and age

Abrams et al 1985 - % attending church monthly			
	<30yrs	*30+ not retired*	*retired*
male	15	16	14
female (working)	25	33	40
female (non-working)	6	36	40
Cox 1987 - % attending church within previous 2 weeks			
	18-39yrs	*40-64yrs*	*65yrs+*
male	12	15	14
female	17	22	27

In Gorer's 1955 study frequent attendance at church was most common among the 65+ age group and least common among the 25–44 age group. Similar results, at least for the older age group, were obtained in the more recent studies by Abrams et al (1985) and Cox (1987), though in both these cases there are significant male–female differences which are obscured by aggregating the results for men and women.

One of the best sources of data on this topic, both because of the nature of the sample and the availability of time-series data, is the annual British Social Attitudes Survey. In the fourteen years since the first survey was conducted, weekly attendance at a place of worship in the 65+ age group has stayed within the range 16–20%, consistently higher than figures for attendance in the adult population as a whole (see Figure 2).

Figure 2 Attendance at place of worship 65+ years age group, 1983–97

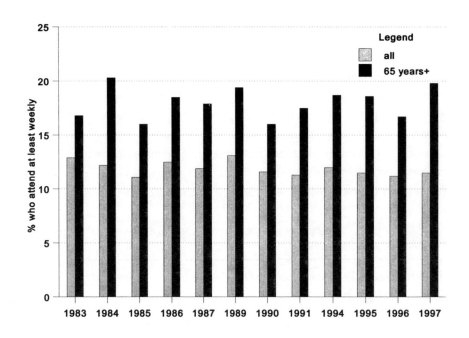

A survey of twenty rural parishes conducted for the Church of England's Archbishops' Commission on Rural Areas found that "the age groups with the highest proportion attending at least once a week are those aged 45–54 and the over 65s" (Davies et al 1991). A somewhat different picture is given, however, by two of the local studies already cited (Owen 1960; Forster 1995). In 1950s Gwynnedd, an area with relatively high levels of attendance, there were fewer frequent attenders in the 60+ age group than in the younger ages (20–60 years). And in Hull, in the late 1980s, an area with relatively low levels of attendance, middle-aged people (30–59 years) were more likely to be regular attenders than other age groups, though the difference was not statistically significant.

Regular attendance is closely associated with age in non-Christian religions also, though as in Hull and Gwynnedd, it is not always the case that the oldest age group contains the highest proportion of regular attenders. In Gunter and Vinery's study it is those in the youngest age group (16–34) among Muslims and Hindus who stand out as the least frequent attenders. Between the two older age groups (35–54; 55+) there is little to choose. Modood and Berthoud (1996) report similar results for Muslim men, with a very slight drop in the proportion of frequent attenders among the 50+ age group. For Muslim women, on the other hand, it is the oldest group who stand out as the most frequent attenders, with little to choose among the two younger age groups. Among Redbridge Jews there are also important differences between the sexes. There is a clear age gradient in regular attendance for men, but not for women (Kosmin and Levy 1978).

Table 2 Regular synagogue attenders as a proportion of
each age group and sex

Age	Males %	Females %
20-29	6.5	9.3
30-39	5.8	7.7
40-49	10.4	7.4
50-59	14.7	5.9
60-69	18.0	8.8
70+	33.3	13.2

The relative positions of different age groups with respect to church attendance is viewed from a somewhat different angle by several studies which compare the proportion of regular attenders in different age groups with the proportion of the general population in those same age groups. One point which emerges very clearly from these studies is the different age structures of different churches.

In York in the early 1950s, 37% of the adult attenders at Anglican churches were aged 50 years or more, only slightly more than the national figure for adults in this age group (35.4%). In York's Nonconformist churches, however, 45% of the adults were in this older age group. The Roman Catholics were by contrast a relatively youthful church with only 23% of adult attenders aged 50 years or more (Rowntree and Lavers 1951). Similar congregational differences were reported in a 1960s Gallup poll survey. Thirteen per cent of the regular attenders at Anglican churches, 14% at Nonconformist churches, but only 4% at Roman Catholic churches were aged 65 years or more. Since the proportion of aged 65 years or more in the whole sample was 8%, the Roman Catholics are once again seen to have youthful congregations wheareas Nonconformist churches (and also this time Anglicans) are more dependent on older people. A local study of two Methodist congregations from the mid-1960s confirms this view (Clark 1970). "The age and sex profile of the two Methodist churches gives a fairly typical local type picture i.e. in both congregations the middle-aged and especially the elderly, notably elderly women, were dominant." The Mormons, by contrast, are a relatively youthful church (Buckle 1971).

The most recent figures for the age structure of different churches is provided by the two MARC Europe censuses (Brierley 1991). The Church of England, the Methodists, the Baptists and the United Reformed Church all have disproportionately elderly congregations and what is more their congregations aged between 1979 and 1989. The big change revealed by these studies is in the age structure of Roman Catholic congregations. In 1989, 16% of Catholic churchgoers were aged 65 years or over, more or less the same as the proportion than in the general population. The relatively youthful churches now are the independents and the Afro-Caribbean churches. When the figures for the different churches are aggregated, as in Table 3, it can be seen that younger adults are under-represented in the churchgoing population and older adults (those 65 years or more) are over-represented.

Older adults are more likely than younger adults to be regular attenders at forms of communal worship. The generalisation holds good of most Christian churches (though there are significant differences between them), and also of Jews (Kosmin and Levy 1978), Muslims and Hindus (Gunter and Vinery 1994). The generalisation also depends heavily on the width of the age bands selected for comparison. Studies which compare people aged 40 years (or 50 years) and over with younger adults provide it with less equivocal support than studies which compare people in narrower age bands. There are, as we have seem, some surveys which show middle-aged people to be the most frequent attenders at a place of worship.

In 1955, two-fifths of the English population made prayer a regular part of their lives, precisely one-third saying prayers daily and 11% more frequently (Gorer 1955). Regular private prayer was much more common among older than younger adults. Twenty-four per cent of people aged 65 years or more prayed more than once a day and 71% at least once a day.

Forty years later, in Hull, Forster (1995) observed a somewhat weaker relationship between age and private prayer. There was hardly any difference in the proportions of older and middle-aged people who said they sometimes prayed privately (60%), though only 23% of the younger age group (17–30) did so. Forster, unlike Gorer, fails to distinguish regular private prayer as a form of devotional activity from intermittent 'crisis prayer' (which was *less* common among older people).

Table 3 Percentage of churchgoers in different age groups compared to general population

Age group	Churchgoers in 1979 Men / Women/ Total			Churchgoers in 1989 Men / Women / Total			Population 1989 Men / Women / Total		
<15	13	13	26	12	13	25	10	9	19
15-19	4	5	9	3	4	7	4	4	8
20-29	5	6	11	4	6	10	8	8	16
30-44	7	9	16	7	10	17	10	10	20
45-64	9	11	20	9	13	22	11	11	22
65+	7	11	18	7	12	19	6	9	15
All ages	45	55	100	42	58	100	49	51	100

Are people who watch or listen to religious broadcasts, especially broadcasts of services, engaging in a private religious activity? Or are they simply watching other people participate in a public religious activity? More older people are regular viewers of religious broadcasts than are regular churchgoers (Coleman 1990). For some older people, especially those with mobility problems, it is possible that religious broadcasts are a substitute for attendance at church. The authors of the 1954 NCSS survey of 100 people aged 70 or more certainly thought so when they drew attention to several non-attenders at church who "listened to services on the wireless ... and one who, unable to listen to broadcast services as she had no wireless, 'lived on her faith'". And viewers themselves think that the "primary aim of religious broadcasting is the provision of services for people who cannot get to church" (Svennegig 1988). In a large general population sample, however, it seems that regular churchgoers are more likely to watch religious programmes than non-attenders or infrequent attenders, "though it is not clear if they watched these programmes mostly when unable to get out" (Gunter and Vinery 1994). Older people do watch more religious programmes on television than younger people (Svennegig 1988), though this may say more about patterns of church attendance than patterns of mobility.

Studies which have asked people about their religious beliefs have reported a similar difference between older and younger adults to those which have asked about practice, though here once again generalisations should be hedged round with qualifications. Investigators have asked about beliefs specific to the Christian creed as well as beliefs shared by the major monotheistic religions (belief in a personal God or belief in an afterlife) and beliefs which are alien to these religions (belief in reincarnation). They have offered respondents the opportunity to distinguish belief in a personal God (the God of Christianity or Judaism or Islam) from other forms of theism (belief in an impersonal 'life force' or Spirit). They have asked about hellfire and the devil. They have even asked about ghosts.

For most of these items (with the possible exception of ghosts), there is a marked tendency for disbelief to be more common among younger adults than older adults. Mass Observation (1947) found that there were twice as many non-believers (in God) among the younger generation (under 40 years). In Gorer's 1955 study, there is a clear age gradient for belief in an afterlife, which increases from 41% in young adults (25–34) to 58% in older adults (65+). Age differences for belief are much less marked, though still apparent. Abrams et al (1985) reports similar age differences for belief in a personal God as well as belief in God (personal or otherwise), for both men and women. Forster (1995) too finds that older adults (61+) are more likely to be 'theists' than either middle-aged (31–60) or younger (17–30) adults.

A somewhat different pattern of age-related differences emerges from a 1963 Gallup poll survey (Martin 1968).

> Belief in immortality like belief in God has a curious age distribution. Belief rises with each age group up to 45–64 years but drops 5% in the 65+ age group.... Do the over 65s show this decline in belief in immortality because the nearer they approach death the more stoically realistic they become? Or is it that this generation, whose youth was dominated by the First World War, suffered losses of faith as well as life in that formative period?

What *is* clear from this survey is that a central item of orthodox Christian belief – belief in a personal God – is more common in older than younger age groups. The modal age for belief in God is 45–64 years; the modal age for belief in a *personal* God is 65+ years.

Combined 'religiosity' or 'religious commitment' scales are used by both Abrams et al (1985) and Svennegig (1988) to make age group comparisons. Both studies show a clear age gradient in their chosen scale, people in older age groups being more religious than those in younger age groups. Both studies agree also in reporting fairly high scores on their measures of religiosity for the majority of older people (65 years+) – 65% in Abrams and 52% in Svennegig. These figures are higher than those reported by the same studies for either regular churchgoing or orthodox belief.

A sense of the importance which people attach to religion (i.e. to their own individual adherence to the beliefs and practices prescribed by organised religion) is tapped in several studies by asking just one or two questions. Would they, for example, describe themselves as religious persons? Is religion important to them or a source of comfort? A study of older people in northeast Scotland found that

> to more than half the older people in our sample religion appeared to be an important value in their lives; though no systematic enquiry in depth was possible, even with generous allowance for any tendency to give 'respectable replies', it was quite clear that Christian faith was a mainstay to a substantial proportion of both sexes, but especially in women. (Richardson 1964)

In another study from northeast Scotland, Reid (1978) reported that 42% of men and 63% of women aged 65 years or more "derived much [rather than merely 'some'] comfort from religion". No doubt these results owe something to the unusual vigour of organised Christianity in this part of Britain in the 1960s and 1970s. Even so, results from more recent studies in other parts of the country suggest that religious practice and/or belief retains some value for at least a large minority of older people. In Southampton, 71% of a sample of elderly people said that religion meant a lot to them (Coleman 1990). In the European Values study, 57% of retired men and 70% of retired women said that God was important in their lives, rather fewer than the proportion of those who defined themselves as religious – 72% of retired men and 70% of retired women (Abrams et al 1985). Copeland (1986) found that well over half of a Liverpool sample of older people claimed that religion was fairly important or very important in their lives. Forster (1995) reports that 57% of older (60+) residents on a Hull council estate claimed to derive comfort and strength from religion; 62% of the respondents in this age group considered themselves to be religious.

Thirty-seven per cent of the over-55s in the most recent of the television surveys (Gunter and Vinery 1994) said that religion was very important in their lives, slightly fewer than those who said that "religious beliefs are a help in facing the problems of life" (42%), and rather more than those who said that "without religious belief life is meaningless" (25%). Among older Muslim, Hindu and Black Pentecostal respondents in the same study the figures were even higher: 80%, 65%, and 98% respectively of these groups said that religion was very important to them. Similar patterns of response for older people (50+) from different ethnic groups was reported by Modood and Berthoud (1996). Where age comparisons are made for responses to these questions about the importance of religion, they support the view that older people are more religious than younger people (Abrams et al 1985; Gunter and Vinery 1994; Forster 1995). Copeland (1986), interestingly enough, found a significant difference in the proportion of 'older old' (69% of 75+ year olds) and 'younger old' (51% of 65–74 year olds) who said that religion was important to them.

Older people, it seems, are more likely than younger people to affirm the importance of organised religion, not only for themselves, but also for the community. This sense of the social utility of the institutions of religion is apparent in many of the surveys cited in this chapter. According to Gunter and Vinery (1994), for example, a firm conviction that "religion helps to maintain the morals and standards of society" was more common among the over-55s (39%) than either the 35–54 year olds (22%) or the 16–34 year olds (14%).

Surveys which ask people about their relation to organised religion, their adherence to institutionally approved practices and beliefs, leave out something which, to the minds of some researchers, might tell us about the religiousness of the British people. Hay and Heald (1987), for example, are interested, not in organised religion, but in "something less tangible – the inner life that most of us rarely share with others". The phenomenon of "religious or transcendental experience" is for them a dimension of religiousness which social researchers ignore at peril of superficiality. Forty-seven per cent of older respondents (65+) in a 1970s NOP omnibus survey (Hay 1990) reported "having been aware of [at least once in their lives] or influenced by a presence or a power, whether referred to as God or not, which was different from their everyday selves". Reports of religious experience were much less common among younger people. Not all respondents gave a religious interpretation to their experience. Fourteen per cent of atheists/agnostics and 11% of people who attached no importance to the spiritual side of life responded positively. Hay himself acknowledges, however, that these results, and those of a 1985 Gallup poll (Hay 1990), provide only specious support for the view that older people are more religious than younger people. The phenomenon may "turn up with more or less equal frequency from adolescence onwards, so that the longer a person has lived, the more likely he is to report it".

ETHNOGRAPHIC STUDIES

No survey of British social research into the connection between religion and ageing would be complete without mention of a handful of ethnographic studies which stand more or less apart from the framework of themes which has determined the structure of this chapter. Studies by Jerrome (1989, 1992), Williams (1990) and Thompson et al (1990) all of which rely on qualitative methods to investigate the ways in which older people construct their social and personal lives are useful, each in their different way, for the light they cast on whether and how the relation of individuals to church and religion gives decisive shape to the experience of ageing. They all have something to say on the nature of the benefits that are conferred on older people by association with organised religion.

Jerrome is interested mainly in the *social* benefits of membership of religious organisations as one kind of voluntary association among others. In a 1989 study of age relations in an English Methodist Church, she suggests that

> compared with older people in other settings, members of the church are privileged in a number of ways. Their presence is crucial for the accomplishment of the various instrumental and expressive goals of the church. They have 'sown seeds', and are invited to see their current, frequently marginal experience in the context of involvement between the generations. They have helped to socialise the young to the demands of the Christian life and through them enjoy a sense of continuity.

The church offers an important illustration of an 'age-mixed' social group in which everyone has a part to play. Also associated with the church were two 'age-graded' organisations, one for men and one for women, Christian fellowships with considerable similarities to secular pensioners' clubs (Jerrome 1992), though there are of course important differences between the two kinds of association – the fellowships are religious organisations and the content of their meetings is largely devotional.

> Fellowship in the sense of spiritual solidarity is sought, rather than friendship. They come for company, to pass the time, and in memory of past glories, of the days when the meeting was one hundred strong and supported a large and famous choir.

Jerrome (1992) wonders whether "the timeless quality" of the meeting, its "contrast to the time-stressed daily routine", enabled the attenders to be free from the pressure, so strongly felt at home, to "manufacture pastimes to avoid feeling alone".

What interests Williams (1990) is the relevance of self-image and world-view to the ability of older people, in this case older Aberdonians with a strong Calvinist legacy, to cope with illness, disability and death. He describes the situation of individuals whose self-image was tied to the "usually approved" qualities – those of being a healthy, active, determined or hard-working person – and for whom irremediable disability implied a "disastrous loss of self". What he calls "conventional churchgoers", older people who were church members but either lacked or failed to express "an organised world view", were in more or less the same boat. Aberdonians who subscribed to "purely ethical or rationalist philosophies" were in a better position than either of these types as they had world views which supplied them with a "wider and more flexible repertoire of responses" to illness. They too, however, appeared to have nothing to draw on when faced with "irreducible illness".

> By contrast older people with world views which centred on some conception of faith not only offered the widest repertoire for coping positively with controllable illness, but also offered resources for dealing positively with irreducible illness.

Thompson and colleagues (1990), using life story interviews with three generations of families in order to describe the strategies by which people find meaning and fulfilment in later life, paint a very different picture from that offered by Williams. To be more specific, they come to different conclusions having asked different kinds of question of a rather different sample. What stands out from the interview material is, firstly, the importance for older people of the ability to maintain "a continuingly meaningful personal way of life" and, secondly, the fact that this ability varies between individuals.

Thompson acknowledges that it is not easy to say what makes for success in this "crucial task". What is clear is that "religious beliefs seem only very rarely to have an important influence in outcome: those who frequent churches see themselves as sustained by the company rather than by the doctrine they offer". Much more important, he thinks, than religious belief are factors like level of education in early life, access to leisure facilities, grand parenting and the intimacy of relationships with others adults.

CONCLUSION

If regular attendance at a place of worship is a reliable indicator of an individual's participation in organised religion, then only a minority of older people in this country can be said to participate in organised religion. Regional differences, as well as differences between urban and rural areas, appear to have decreased in recent years (Brierley 1991), though by all accounts, the people of Northern Ireland remain exceptionally loyal to their various churches (Greeley 1992). What is true of the older population as a whole is not true, however, of some of the larger minority ethnic groups, especially those from South Asia. Only a very small minority of South Asians say that they are without a religion and levels of religious observance for the majority are relatively high (Modood and Berthoud 1996).

There are, however, various reasons for questioning whether participation in communal worship is a reliable indicator of personal involvement in organised religion. Some religious groups, for example, attach more importance than others to regular participation in communal worship. It is notoriously possible to attend religious services regularly for reasons which have little to do with religion. Rowntree and Lavers (1951) cite various examples among the older churchgoers they interviewed in York: one man who attends regularly "but does not take it seriously"; another "who does not consider himself religious but will go to church if the weather is fine"; another who goes only "to please his wife"; and another who went to the Cathedral "but only for the music". It is also possible to withdraw from participation in communal worship and yet retain a strong and active attachment to religion through private prayer or Bible reading or watching religious services on television.

In the USA, Mindel and Vaughan (1978) looked at what they called "non-organizational aspects of religious participation" among older people, and found, especially for those people who would be counted amongst the 'older-old', that "religion is still a salient factor in their lives ... despite *declining* participation in formally organized worship". Ainsley and Smith (1984) similarly found that a declining in communal worship was offset by an increase in private religious activities. In the UK, as we have seen, there is very little evidence, and certainly very little evidence from recent years, about the private religious activities of older people and the extent to which they may come to replace, rather than complement, public religious activities. On balance, however, it seems very unlikely that more than a minority of older people maintain their attachment to the Christian religion through private or domestic devotions, since only a minority of older people have such an attachment to maintain. Outside Christianity things may be slightly different, especially for older women (see for example, Michaelson 1987; Modood and Berthoud 1996).

Although only a minority of older people in the UK are churchgoers or profess attachment to the beliefs of the Christian churches, religious beliefs are avowed by a majority. Some of these people will of course profess attachment to other well-defined religions. Most of them, however, appear to be institutionally unattached. It is not at all clear what this says about the religiousness of older people. Or indeed of the majority of the adult population who say that they believe in God (Abrams et al 1985) and that it is "necessary" for them to have religious belief (Svennegig 1988). The view expressed by Rowntree and Lavers in 1951, that these majority beliefs, far from being oddly disconnected fragments in a thoroughly secularised outlook, indicate the presence of "a real though seldom expressed hunger for supernatural religion" finds an echo in the comments of a more recent researcher, who wonders whether the evidence points to "the opening of a gulf between established religions and people's needs for spiritual guidance" (Svennegig 1988).

Such affirmations of the importance of religious belief have to be squared with the fact that declarations even of orthodox belief may have limited personal significance for the people who make them. Speaking of a large national sample of Roman Catholics (of all ages), Hornsby-Smith (1991) says that

> their religion had salience for only a tiny minority of our ordinary Catholics, even where they were regular mass attenders. Their outlook was generally this-worldly and pragmatic, and this was reflected in the strength of the movement towards 'making up your own mind' especially on issues of personal morality.

Hornsby-Smith's tiny minority stands in clear contrast with the findings of those questionnaire surveys which suggest that religion plays an important part in the lives of a majority of older people in this country. Evidently the importance of religion to the individual may be assessed in different ways.

Hornsby-Smith's measure of 'salience' corresponds to what the American sociologists Stark and Glock (1968) called the "consequential dimension of religiosity, that is, the effects of religious belief, practice, experience and knowledge on people's day-to-day-lives". The requirements of salience in this sense are fairly high: religion must be seen to make a difference to the way people live their lives. To demonstrate the salience of religion for older people, it is not enough to ask them *whether* religion is important in their lives; it is necessary to determine *what* it is that they are talking about and *how* it is important in their lives. This is not to say that Hornsby-Smith's findings undermine the other material presented in this chapter on the self-perceived importance of religion. This material does *suggest* that religion plays an important part in the lives of a large minority, if not a majority, of older people – more at any rate than those who regularly attend public worship or accept the creeds of church religion. With some older people, those for example who say that they pray and read the Bible every day, it is relatively easy to understand what they mean when they affirm the importance of religion for how they live their lives. When, on the other hand, claims for the importance of religion are made by people who appear to have detached themselves from the practices *and beliefs* of organised religion, it is less easy to understand what they mean without further inquiry.

Claims for the self-perceived importance of religion, however they are to be understood, are more likely to be made by older people than younger people. The same holds for avowals of religious belief and religious observance. Do these well-documented age differences in religiousness say something about the way people tend to change as they get older (a life cycle effect)? Or do they tell us only about the differences between different generations in a period of cultural change? Over the course of this century succeeding generations in this country have moved away from organised religion. Under such circumstances it is only to be expected that members of older generations will be more attached to religion than younger adults. They are, so to speak, 'survivors of a bygone age', when the experience of Sunday school in childhood was still widespread, even among the children of people who were not themselves regular churchgoers.

The desire to ascertain whether "the primary concern of the elderly in our society is religion and preparation for death"(Blazer and Palmore 1976) has prompted a not inconsiderable number of US studies into the place of religion in later life. Researchers have wanted to put to the test the "common assumption that as people get older they become more religious" (Markides 1983). It is relatively easy to cite evidence which suggests that something of this kind is *expected* of older people, though less so in the 'here and now' than for earlier times and other places (for example, Amoss and Harrell 1981; Cole 1992) It is also relatively easy to understand why it should be that disengagement from an active social life and a sense of declining physical powers or the imminence of death might make a difference to the individual's everyday preoccupations and intensify religious concerns. And if inclinations change, so do opportunities. Freedom from wage-earning and child-rearing may be freedom to devote oneself to aims for which the practical demands of daily life had previously left no time. The story sounds plausible enough, especially if we think of people who, in early adulthood and middle-age, remain attached to the religion in which they were raised, but in a rather 'superficial' or conventional way, the sort of person whose religion does not extend much beyond minimal conformity to prescribed observances and creeds, without any 'far reaching implications for what they feel and think and do about all aspects of their situation in life'. But is this what really happens? And even if it is true that people who are already religious (in this sense) grow more religious as they grow older, is there an analogous intensification of religious leanings among the majority of people who believe without belonging (Davie 1994)?

The evidence from the UK survey data is far too thin to provide robust answers to these questions. There is plenty of evidence to suggest that older people are more religious than younger people (though not all the evidence points this way;

the burdens of old age may subject religious beliefs to intolerable strains). There is also plenty of evidence to suggest that attachment to institutional religion is declining, so that what is true of the present older generation may not be true of future generations. To date, however, there are no UK longitudinal studies which look at changes in religious commitment over time (the exception is Wadsworth and Freeman [1983] who look at change in younger adults). Also most of the studies cited in this chapter have taken a fairly extended view of who is to count as an older person; the comparisons between young and old in the earlier Gallup surveys and the more recent IBA surveys cover very wide age bands. They do not tell us much, for example, about the differences between people in their fifties and those in their sixties and seventies.

The US evidence, which is more copious and wide-ranging than the UK data, to some extent helps to make up for these deficiencies. An abundance of cross-sectional studies from the USA confirm that older adults are more likely to be regular churchgoers than younger adults (Moberg 1965, 1993). Attendance drops off, however, among the older old, though private religious activities do not. Here, it seems, is a clear example of a life cycle effect. Social participation in religious groups appears to increase in line with the opportunities presented by retirement from paid employment. In later years it declines, not because of loss of interest, but presumably because of increasing ill-health and loss of mobility.

Results from longitudinal studies confirm the decline in religious attendance in late old age and cast some doubt on the view that religious concerns intensify with age. Blazer and Palmore (1976), analysing results from the first Duke Longitudinal Study of Aging, report a general decline in church attendance over an eighteen-year period, from the mid-1950s to the 1970s. The median age of the sample at the time of the first interview was 70.8 years. Levels of churchgoing were relatively high, even for the USA, though they had been higher still during the childhood of the respondents. Religious attitudes ("religion is a great comfort", "my religion is very important to me"), on the other hand, remained stable over the same period. In other words, in late old age when the restrictions of ill-health become more and more pressing, there was no sign of any intensification of religious concern. More or less the same conclusions were reached by Markides and Levin (1987) after an eight-year follow-up study.

There is little evidence that older people turn increasingly to religion as they age and approach death. The data showed that indicators of religiosity remained fairly stable over time, with the possible exception of church attendance, which declined slightly among the very old.

Once again the mean age of the sample at the beginning of the study was fairly high (70 years). The bearing of these results on the question of a life cycle effect depends therefore on the location of that effect in late old age, a time of accelerating physical decline. Even so, it is with these results in mind that we should consider what inferences are to be drawn from Copeland's (see above) cross-sectional comparison of the self-perceived importance of religion among the older old and the younger old.

These two studies by themselves hardly suffice, however, to settle the issue about the significance of observed age differences in religious commitment and concern. Beit-Hallahmi and Argyle (1997), in a review of evidence, argue that age differences in church attendance should be put down to historical changes – older people had acquired their faith when society was more religious. On the other hand, they seem willing to accept that observed differences in religious belief, especially belief in an afterlife, and also private devotionalism may reflect a genuine life cycle effect. Moberg (1993), in another review, comes to a different conclusion: "The explanation that stands up best is that the aging process itself contributes to a deepening of religious concern, especially on the private non-organisational level." Slater (1995) agrees. "Older individuals are more involved in religious matters than the young, and this appears to have been the case for long enough for us to suppose that it is not simply a generational effect." That succeeding generations differ from each other need not be doubted. Nor can it be doubted that the second half of this century has seen a weakening of the authority of organised religion. It is quite a different matter, however, to show that observed age differences in religious belief are *no more* than a generational effect.

2

THE CHURCHES AND OLDER PEOPLE: SOCIAL POLICIES AND SOCIAL ACTION

The last fifty years have seen a continuing process of reassessment by the Christian churches in Britain of the nature and extent of their responsibilities towards older people. When they have taken up the situation of older people in various official and semi-official reports and surveys, more often than not it has been because of a need to reconsider the kind of practical response that is demanded from them by what is seen to be new in this situation. This chapter will examine some of the ways in which the 'demands of the situation' have been formulated and re-formulated in recent years. Most of the documents that will be cited come from Christian churches. Analogous documentary material for non-Christian groups other than the Jewish community is very thin on the ground. Words and ideas, rather than actions, are the main subject of interest, and it would of course be wrong to infer from the public silence of the institutional representatives of a particular religious community that the community concerns itself very little with the well-being of older people.

This chapter begins by illustrating some of the ideas which form the framework, far from fixed admittedly, within which any discussion of the obligations of churches' towards older people should be set. In 1924 the Church of England established an independent housing trust, Church Army Housing, to provide housing for "people of limited means irrespective of colour, race or creed". It was also established in order "to demonstrate the Church as a caring body concerned with the whole of life – material and spiritual". People without decent housing, like people without enough to eat, have a 'material' need which the community as a whole including the churches should try to do something about. In accepting an obligation to help with the provision of housing in England in the 1920s, the Church was showing a determination not to restrict its sense of responsibility to the spiritual side of life, to what might be considered as its own special sphere of competence as a religious institution; and in dissociating the provision from any kind of religious qualification, it was also accepting an obligation, in the language characteristic of Christian thinking on this matter, to serve the whole community. It was demonstrating what is now called 'Christian social concern' by adding to a common stock the same kinds of resources as are possessed by purely secular agencies.

The author of a 1990 report on the churches and community work writes that "the Church, by its own self-definition, is a caring body, and this is appropriately manifested through its activities" (Ballard 1990). What this means, as official pronouncements like that of the Church of England on Church Army Housing are often at pains to emphasise, is that they care for the 'whole person – spiritual *and* material'. In other words, they should not restrict their responsibilities to their distinctive role as a religious institution, which is the preservation and transmission of religious teachings and the 'nourishment of the spiritual life' of members.

However matters stood in 1924, there seems little doubt that in the 1990s, the relationship between the expression of 'Christian social concern' and the distinctive role of churches as religious institutions often has been fraught with difficulty (Ballard 1990). It is not hard to see why. It is one thing for the churches to care for the whole person, material and spiritual, when the people concerned are their own members. It is quite a different matter when the people concerned are of another faith or no faith.

In a society where various religious communities are embedded within a wider and largely secularised society, individual members of a religious community share with each other beliefs and values which they do not share with the wider society. These beliefs and values shape their sense of what they owe to each other and also their sense of what the church as an institution owes to them. The members of such a community share a common understanding of what it is to show proper concern for the whole person – spiritual and material. They expect that the institutions of the community will not restrict the exercise of their pastoral responsibilities towards members of their congregations to the spiritual side of life, even while recognising that the spiritual side of life is, after all, its special sphere of competence. When, on the other hand, the churches, look outwards to the wider society, there is an inevitable tension between the way in which they express their social concern and their distinctive role as (Christian) religious institutions. There is, in the words of the British Council of Churches' report, "a risk that 'the world set the agenda' ... a proper anxiety that the churches' particular contribution will be obscured" (Ballard 1990). When the 'world sets the agenda', the churches allow their concern for the welfare of the wider society to be channelled exclusively into meeting those needs which the whole of society can agree to recognise and make provision for. And if this is allowed to happen, although they will continue to have a distinctive role to play – a special sphere of competence – in their own communities, in the wider society this distinctive role may be lost to sight.

The churches are interested in older people, first and foremost, because they see themselves as having obligations towards them. The 1986 report of the Church of England Archbishops' Commission on Urban Priority Areas, *Faith in the city*, sets out these obligations in their broadest terms when it describes a church as a special kind of community. A local church is a religious community "constituted by people in a certain town or area, who meet together regularly, bear one another's burdens, suffer one another's pain and participate in a common celebration". It aspires to be a community in which "every individual matters ... and each person's gift is given full opportunity to be exercised". This local community, simply by virtue of the fact it has older people as members, should ask itself what can and should be done to share their burdens and what is to be done to ensure that its older members continue to have "full opportunity to exercise their gift" despite their age. A Christian community should not, however, be purely inward-looking. It should be "open to, and responsible for the whole of the society in which it is set, and proclaims its care for the weak, its solidarity with all, and its values which lie beyond the mere satisfaction of material needs". In other words, the church "proclaims its care" for older people 'in their weakness', whether they are inside or outside of the church as a local community.

The conception of the Church, or a church, as a special kind of community is not peculiar to the Church of England of course. It is a widely disseminated idea with a long tradition, though it seems, for various reasons no doubt, to have gained a new life in post-war years (see, for example, Hornsby-Smith 1989 for a discussion of the 'quest for community' in recent Catholic thinking). It provides a useful counterpoint to the idea of a church as a powerful and hierarchical institution and serves as a reminder that there is more to 'full participation in the life of the church' than regular attendance at a ritual celebration. Community-building has indeed become a very salient feature in the moral thinking of some of the mainstream churches (witness *Faith in the city* and the Catholic Bishops' response to the 1980 National Pastoral Congress): the churches as institutions should strive to transform their congregations into real Christian communities. Members are enjoined to transform ideals into social reality and to become 'model' communities to be emulated by the wider society in which they are set – an injunction inspired by the sense that secular society is becoming increasingly deficient in important respects. The distinction between the church as a 'community of believers' and the church as an institution which regulates and cares for that community is of fundamental importance for any discussion of the social policy of the churches. The church as a community cares, or should care, for its members *inter alia* by being a source of reciprocal social support and mutual aid. When the church as the institutional expression of organised religion offers the same kind of care, it is acting as a social welfare agency with delegated responsibilities.

The mere presence of older people within the churches and outside of them is sufficient therefore to generate obligations. The churches have these obligations as collectivities which aspire to a certain ideal of 'community', as institutions which claim authority and competence in their own special province, and as organisations with widely varying degrees of influence and power which may present significant opportunities for social action in the wider community. Inevitably the way in which these obligations are exercised will change as circumstances change. The idea of a Christian community as it is presented in *Faith in the city* already acknowledges one large change in the circumstances in which the churches must exercise their obligations towards older people: it is no longer possible for them to act as though the Christian community comprised the whole of society. It is also important, however, to look into ways in which the social situation of older people, as well as society's understanding of that situation, has been transformed in recent decades. And that is the topic of this chapter. How have the churches understood the demands made upon them by the changing situation of older people? What is it that has demanded a practical response from them and how have they responded?

CHURCH VOLUNTARY ACTION AND THE WELFARE STATE

In the Britain of the late 1940s the social landscape was radically changed by the new institutions of the welfare state. The post-war Labour government resolved that no-one should be reliant on private charity for essential material goods like food, clothing and decent accommodation and established the appropriate institutions. No older person therefore should be forced to turn to the churches for help with their material needs. ("Philanthropy", as Crossman recalled later in 1976, "was to us the odious expression of social oligarchy and churchy bourgeois attitudes.") What did this mean for the churches' responsibilities to older people, members and non-members? Had they been relieved of their responsibilities for the 'material' side of life by statutory provisions for pensions and the new institutions for providing social services? Would they no longer be required to care for the "whole person – spiritual and *material*", even within their own communities? Should they now, in the words of a 1961 report looking at the implications of these developments for the churches, "devote their energies to the intensive cultivation of the personal spiritual life of their adherents?" (Birmingham Council of Churches 1961).

As it happens, the churches appear not to have been much exercised by these questions during the early infancy of the welfare state. What was required to rouse them to active consideration of the issues was observation, over several years, of the working effectiveness of the new institutions under conditions of social change. By the second half of the 1950s it had become clear to many observers that the statutory services were overstretched and lacked the resources to meet the demands of the situation. Nor, so it was argued, could the problem be solved simply by expanding these services. If the churches had thought, or hoped, that the new welfare state would relieve them of their responsibilities for the material side of life, events had proved them wrong.

WELL-DEFINED ROLES AND WELL-DEFINED NEEDS?

The first phase in the process of reassessment by the churches of their responsibilities towards older people corresponds then to the period of the early development of the welfare state. During this period the churches (considered collectively) pursued activities to which they still attach importance and which constitute a response to three distinct kinds of need in the older population: the need for suitable accommodation; the need for companionship; and the need to maintain contact with the church in the performance of its religious ministry. What is distinctive about these activities is that they did not encroach upon the sphere of competence claimed by the institutions of the new welfare state.

Beveridge (1948), writing about voluntary action for social welfare, reiterates the conclusions of the earlier Nuffield report on older people (Rowntree 1947), when he singles out some of the special needs of old age which were beyond the reach of the new welfare state. Of particular importance for his own chosen theme were the need for suitable accommodation and the need for companionship; for from the existence of these limitations he concluded that there was plenty of scope for voluntary action to improve the welfare of older people. And although Beveridge himself was not very sanguine about the capacity of the churches in this regard (seeing them as institutions with declining power and influence), they were active nevertheless in meeting both kinds of need.

The provision of housing is of course quite a different matter from the provision of companionship. There is a good case for arguing that responsibility for meeting people's needs for companionship should not be delegated to specialist agencies, statutory or otherwise, which does not apply to the provision of housing. And when the post-war government encouraged religious organisations, as well as other voluntary agencies, to continue as providers of residential care, it was because these agencies already had resources and expertise in the field (Brenton 1985). They were invited to cast themselves in a new role as paid agents of the welfare state rather than dispensers of private charity. The government could hardly spurn the efforts of voluntary providers on the grounds of amateurism when their own provision was so open to criticism on grounds of quality. The 1947 Nuffield Foundation survey of the social conditions of old people favourably compares with the facilities provided by statutory authorities those which were pioneered by Catholic and Anglican religious sisterhoods as well as those of the Salvation Army (Rowntree 1947).

How did these religious providers of residential accommodation for older people conceive of their role? Were they offering something to members of the religious community with which they were associated, something which expressed their concern for "the whole of life – material and spiritual"? Or was the offer extended to any older person in the wider community? The answer, in some cases at least, is that they were doing both. They recognised an obligation to do something to meet the needs of their members for specialised housing in later life. They endeavoured to offer to *some* of their members who could no longer live independently an opportunity to reside in a communal home, with a shared view of how to show proper concern for the whole of human life, material *and spiritual*. The offer, however, was not confined to the members of their own particular religious community, even if in practice most of the residents belonged to this community (there are still very few non-Catholics in homes run by Catholic religious orders). The distinguishing feature of these religious providers such as Methodist Homes for the Aged and various Roman Catholic religious orders such as the Little Sisters of the Poor, the Sisters of Nazareth and the Order of St John is not so much a religious qualification on residency as the *ethos* which underlies provision.

Alongside the religious providers who extended their offer of residential care beyond the limits of their own religious community, there were other facilities set up by churches or other religious organisations which did cater exclusively for members of the particular religious communities which supported their work. Of twenty-one 'rest homes' listed in a 1965 guide to housing provided by the Church of England, ten required residents to be communicants of the Church. Although such exclusivity may be rarer now than it was thirty years ago, it still occurs. There are a few organisations which provide special accommodation for elderly members of the Protestant churches (for example, Pilgrim Homes). The Jewish community is also conspicuous for the efforts it makes to provide separate residential care for its own members through Jewish Care, the specialist Jewish social services agency, through Nightingale Homes, and most recently, the Otto Fisch Foundation, established originally to provide accommodation for refugees from central Europe. These organisations do more than provide residential care to people who are no longer able to live independently in the community. They offer the opportunity to live in a community whose identity is formed by shared religious beliefs and values. More emphatically even than those homes that are open to outsiders, the communal home is, or aspires to be, a living fragment of the religious community which it serves. The provider sees itself as having no obligation to offer a place to an 'outsider' who does not identify with the community and has no desire to participate in its distinctive shared life; on the contrary its first obligation is to those who understand themselves to be part of the community which the home serves.

There has of course been a great deal of change and expansion of voluntary sector housing provision for older people since the 1940s. According to Wistow and colleagues (1996) much of the residential care provided by religious organisations is more open to outsiders than it used to be. No longer should they be thought of as serving the community from which they sprang; rather "they retain an orientation and cultivate an ethos which reflects their religious group focus" (though as we have seen, at least some of the large religious providers have always been open in principle to outsiders). The sector has also seen a shift towards the provision of self-contained accommodation. Some of this, in the form of sheltered housing, remains closely associated with the organisations which provide other kinds of specialised accommodation for older people. Much of it, however, is provided through housing associations; and although about one half of the housing associations set up since the 1960s were the results of initiatives by Christians, they were intended, from the outset, to meet housing need in the wider community rather than to provide suitable accommodation for their own members (NFHA 1995). And as a report from the Joseph Rowntree Trust (Walker 1994) made clear, religious organisations – many of which own unused or under-used property – are still seen as an important source of growth and diversity in the development of special needs housing.

In recent years, it seems that some Christian providers have been forced to reassess their role as providers of residential care to older people, especially when they have seen themselves as having a twofold role: offering to members of the religious community with which they associated a form of residential care which expressed their concern for the whole of life, material and spiritual; and also making an 'offer of service' to all older persons in the wider community irrespective of their religious beliefs. Providers have been forced to consider how they should demonstrate concern for the spiritual side of life in circumstances when they can no longer take for granted a shared understanding based in shared religious beliefs and values, or perhaps a passive acceptance of how this is to be done. This in turn raises the question whether they should make a deliberate effort to provide residential care which maintains a relatively undiluted commitment to a shared Christian life.

If the post-war government was quick to recognise that continuing voluntary sector provision was to be welcomed, at least as far as housing was concerned, the churches (and other religious organisations) themselves recognised that they had a responsibility to ensure that the sick and the housebound should not be isolated from the religious community. Home visits to older people who find it difficult to get out of the house have long been an acknowledged pastoral responsibility of ministers of religion. Clergy may be called on to perform religious rites for people who are unable to attend services; or to give spiritual counsel where it is felt to be needed; or they may wish simply to show that "the church is a caring body". It is not only ministers of religion who make home visits, however. In the Roman Catholic Church, for example, there are two voluntary societies – the Society of St Vincent de Paul and the Legion of Mary – whose members undertake regular visiting as a kind of 'lay ministry'. And in other churches also lay members of the congregation were, and still are, urged to make friendly visits to older people who could not easily get to church; and it is in this role of course that members of churches can do something about the need for companionship experienced by some older people. When churches engage in home visiting, whether to exercise special spiritual functions or simply to provide companionship, and especially when the visits are in practice restricted to members of their own religious community, it is evident that they are not attempting to meet needs for which the government has shouldered responsibility through the establishment of the welfare state. They are clearly playing their proper part in society and are showing themselves to be caring communities, caring for the whole person, without encroaching on the province of government.

Early post-war surveys of the social situation of older people confirm the importance of the efforts made by the churches to keep in touch with people who were more or less housebound. Rowntree (1947) alludes to "evidence that visits from ministers of religion and from laymen mean a great deal in the lives of many old people"; a Merseyside survey suggested that it was "difficult to assess the amount of friendly visiting of old people ... as a great deal is done by religious organisations ... of which no record is kept" (Black and Read 1947); and in Sheffield it was thought that "the fellowship of a church was of great importance to many people" (Greenlees and Adams 1949). The most recent source of national data for clergy visiting appears be the 1978 Office of

Population Censuses and Surveys (OPCS) survey of the Elderly at Home (Hunt 1978) which found that 16.2% of the sample, with large regional variation, had been visited at home in the previous six months. At least once a fortnight 2.2% of the elderly people in the sample – 5.7% of the housebound elderly – received visits.

Are home visits by the official representatives of a religious community confined to people who are clearly identifiable as members of the community in question? The OPCS figures, based on a nationally representative sample, certainly suggest that the clergy are concentrating their attention on identifiable members of their own religious communities. One important difference between an active rather than nominal member of a religious community, or indeed an outsider, is that the former is more likely to welcome the visit as an occasion for the exercise of functions which lie within the clergy's special sphere of competence. Why, after all, should ministers of religion be obliged to make a home visit in circumstances which make it unlikely that they will be called upon to exercise their distinctive role as ministers of religion?

In a 1964 survey of older people in South Shields over one-fifth of the non-churchgoers in the sample received visits from clergy (Hanson 1964). Tunstall (1966), on the other hand, remarks that there was little evidence of non-attending old people receiving domestic visits from ministers of religion. It is essential in considering evidence of this kind to bear in mind the differences between different churches or denominations.

The Roman Catholic Church in the UK, like the Anglican Church, assigns clergy to geographically-defined parishes. And although, in canon law, the parish priests have pastoral responsibilities towards everyone living within the boundaries of the parish (Ward 1961), in practice they are concerned only with known Catholics in the area. A study of a large Roman Catholic parish in Liverpool (Ward 1961) concluded that "the personal relationship which existed between the priests of the parish and the parishioners was the most single important factor in the social structure of the parish. This relationship appeared to derive to a considerable extent from the regular six-weekly visit of the priests to the homes of [all] the parishioners." A priest had visited 84% of the parishioners (i.e. Catholics living within the parish boundaries) in the six weeks prior to their interview. A list of streets was read out at Mass every Sunday and the priest visited all the Catholic homes in those streets during the week. Visits to the sick and the housebound were more frequent, once a week, and the dying were visited every day.

A similar picture of the role played by home visiting in Roman Catholic pastoral care was painted by Rex and Moore (1967) in their study of immigrant communities in Birmingham in the late 1960s.

> The RC priests, assisted by the Society of St Vincent de Paul and the Legion of Mary, engage in extensive pastoral visitation in Sparkbrook. The priest and the Legion are hampered by the Irish population's mobility, but their work consists mainly of keeping in touch with the immigrant Irish, encouraging them to use only suitable lodgings, to live a life in keeping with the moral expectations of the Church and to maintain religious observances.

Extensive pastoral visitation was also found to characterise the main denominations in a survey of older people (a representative sample) in what is admittedly a rather atypical part of Britain – Armagh in Northern Ireland (Williamson 1975). In the sample 42% of the Catholics, 65% of the Anglicans, 51% of the Presbyterians, and 80% of the Methodists had been visited by a clergyman in the previous month. The higher visitation rates were found among the smaller denominations, i.e. those with a more favourable ratio of clergy to members.

These surveys do not tell us how successful the churches were in keeping in touch with those among their members who had become housebound, though they do give some indication of the degree of importance that some churches would attach to this aspect of their pastoral responsibilities. What the surveys do strongly suggest is variation – variation between different religious groups in their commitment to this activity and variation over time. What also emerges from the survey data is that a significant proportion of older people are dissatisfied with the frequency of the visits they receive from ministers of religion. Conor Ward (1961), for example, in his Liverpool study cites elderly couples who speak regretfully of the time when the priest used to visit at least once a month, before the construction of a new housing estate which increased the population within the parish. Richardson (1964), in a survey in northeast Scotland, wondered whether the churches were failing to maintain sufficiently regular or intimate contact with disabled elderly members. Similar complaints about the frequency of home visiting were made in two surveys from the 1980s: one looking at elderly Jewish people in South London (Jimack 1983) and the other a national survey of Roman Catholics (Hornsby-Smith 1989). Hornsby-Smith, writing twenty-eight years after the study of Liverpool Catholics, comments that

> in Britain at any rate ... there has been a substantial and almost universal decline in the visiting of parishioners in their own homes by priests in recent decades. In retrospect the six-weekly cycle of visiting reported by Ward was a unique

characteristic of some parishes in Liverpool in the early post-war years, but it would be quite misleading to regard it as typical of the parish situation in contemporary Britain. In the national survey [for this study] English Catholics rated their priests rather poorly on this aspect of their work.

Visits by clergy to parishioners or church members in their own homes serve to maintain personal contact between the members of a religious community and the official representatives of the church as an institution. For some individuals who find it hard to get about outside their own homes they may help to mitigate a sense of isolation. The primary function of visits by the clergy is, however, the exercise of pastoral care, and however this is to be understood, it is clearly not the same thing as meeting the need for companionship. The minister or priest or rabbi is visiting in a professional capacity. How successful were, and are, the churches in securing the assistance of their lay members in visiting older people, not only as auxiliaries in the exercise of pastoral care but as 'friendly visitors' willing to spend time responding to what Beveridge called 'the need for companionship'?

As already mentioned, quite a lot of the home visiting that is undertaken by people is an extension of the pastoral work of the clergy. This applies, for example, to much of the work undertaken by the Society of St Vincent de Paul, whose 18,000 members in England and Wales are estimated to have made about one million visits in 1997, mostly to older people (personal communication); and to lay Catholics who take the Blessed Sacrament already consecrated by the priest to people who are housebound; and to Methodists who may take recordings of sermons. It would be wrong, however, to draw too firm a distinction between auxiliary pastoral care undertaken by lay people and friendly visiting. Hornsby-Smith (1989) cites an article about the work of the Society of St Vincent de Paul from a northern parish magazine:

> The majority of the people we visit are elderly and their greatest need is for company and a sympathetic ear so we try, if possible, to visit them on a weekly basis. During the year three social evenings are held.... These are quite simple functions but for many of the people we visit they are the only social functions they attend.

Much of the visiting that goes on is informal, which is to say that no records are kept. One ought not to suppose, however, the ideals of a caring community are easily put into practice or everywhere realised to the same degree. Several of the clerical respondents in an unpublished survey from 1962 (London School of Hygiene and RCN) of the welfare activities of the churches in Buckinghamshire commented on the difficulties experienced in persuading members of the congregation to take on this kind of activity. Ward (1961) contrasted the loyalty shown by individual Catholics to the institution of the church with the loyalty shown to the religious community. Respondents frequently commented on the lack of community spirit. There was a small nucleus of parishioners (about 25%) who were active in church-based voluntary work and only a small minority of these volunteers were engaged in home visiting. This nucleus of active parishioners also formed what Ward called a primary social group among the parishioners. Outside the nucleus there was little evidence of any kind of social interaction between the parishioners except when they were brought together at church functions.

A more up-to-date and, at the same time, more positive view of friendly visiting is presented in the report of the Faith in Elderly People Project (1991) in Leeds and Bradford. Forty-two per cent of the churches in the areas under study replied to a questionnaire about their activities and most of these (72/85) "had an informal system whereby church members visit those who are known to be housebound or in special need of company".

COMMUNITY-BUILDING AND NEIGHBOURHOOD CARE

It was, then, mainly as providers of residential care and sources of companionship for older people that the churches were active in their demonstration of social concern for older people in the immediate post-war years. Although members of the various religious communities served by the churches as institutions were not the sole beneficiaries of this activity, it is not unlikely that in practice they were the main beneficiaries. By the end of the 1950s, however, there are clear signs of a sense of growing pressure, of the need to do more. There was above all a growing awareness of unmet need for practical support and care among older people living independently in the community. The realisation grew that the institutions of the welfare state were overstretched and that this was partly at least due to demographic change. It was a time also when the institutionalisation of older people in residential homes began to acquire clear definition as a major problem for social policy (Townsend 1962). How, in these circumstances, should the churches exercise their social responsibilities towards older people? This second phase in the process of reassessment by the churches of their responsibilities towards older people is characterised by a preoccupation with community-building and neighbourhood care.

One form in which practical support may be offered by the churches to older people locally is the distribution of charitable relief. If the activities of the churches as providers of residential care and sources of companionship for older people do not encroach upon the sphere of competence claimed by the new institutions of the welfare state, the same cannot be said however of the distribution of charitable relief to the poor and needy. The 1962 report on the role of the churches in the field of social welfare in Buckinghamshire observed that there was "little doubt that dispensing charitable funds to the poor and needy of the parish is no longer a major activity of the churches". There was (certainly in the eyes of the respondents to this survey) less poverty around. Perhaps also, it seemed that the relief of financial hardship, unlike the provision of housing, was the proper and exclusive responsibility of the state and an improper area for private charity. Even so, 80% of the informants had discretionary funds at their disposal which they had drawn on in the previous year. "Old people were the most frequent recipients and it was certainly among this section of the community that the churches were aware of most hardship."

Old people were also the most frequent recipients of gifts of food, clothing and coal, usually made at Christmas, Easter and Harvest Festival. At the end of the 1960s, in Banbury, the Catholic Social Services Organisation, the Society of St Vincent de Paul, was still distributing money (raised at retiring collections every Sunday) to older people "in cases of genuine hardship". Most of their help went to Catholics but sometimes money was given to others (Lowe 1969). Although the Society of St Vincent de Paul still offers spiritual *and* material support as and when necessary (and still distributes considerable amounts of money to needy parishioners), there seems little doubt that what was true in 1962 – that the 'dispensation of private charitable relief' (i.e. money) is not a major activity of the churches – is still true in 1999. Certainly it played little part, for instance, in the 1985 proposals of the Church of England for tackling poverty in the inner cities.

In spite of the continuing distribution of charitable relief by the churches well in to the 1960s and beyond, the problem which forced itself upon their notice in the late 1950s and 1960s was not so much the need for financial assistance as the need for the kind of practical support which we now call informal care. Speaking in 1958 of the social conditions of the elderly, Thomas Rudd, a Roman Catholic geriatrician, wrote that "we are faced with a mass of need, greatly outweighing the facilities available to deal with it.... The case of the frail and unwanted elderly person, capable of being managed at home, but for whom the community has no real use, is surely one of the grave moral problems of the day" (Rudd 1958). Although it was important to expand existing facilities and provide more of the professionalised services that were required, the size of the problem was such that "any organised plan to cover the entire need would involve the employment of so many people that the country's economy would be disrupted". Nor was it enough to support by gifts of money the work of voluntary organisations in the field; every citizen has a responsibility to look to the welfare of his or her neighbours. The problem, as Rudd conceived it, is a *moral* one. In other words, it is the proper concern of everyone in the community, and should not be reduced to a problem of *policy* for the agencies of government.

Ten years later, in the introduction to a report on the churches' role in the care of the elderly in Banbury, the same point is set within the context of demographic and social changes which are today a familiar preamble to discussions of social policy and older people. More than seven million people "are now over pensionable age and are facing the problems which extended life brings in a society where mobility has grown, family and community ties have been increasingly broken and where state provision is on a scale never conceived possible fifty years ago.... Our society is only just beginning to recognise the size of the problem presented by this new situation" (Lowe 1969).

One of the most detailed and influential of the responses to the problem of unmet need is to be found in a 1961 report from the Birmingham Council of Churches, an ecumenical group of Anglican and other Protestant Churches. The Birmingham Social Responsibility Project had been set up in the late 1950s to consider the implications of the "new social service state" for the welfare activities of the city's churches. The specific questions which the inquiry sought to answer concerned:

1.   the extent of unmet need, and the new initiatives which churches and voluntary organisations might take to provide for such need as still remains in spite of existing services ('need' is here used to cover, not only material necessities, but also less tangible but important factors making for happiness and well-being);

2.   the extent to which the attitudes of individual citizens towards one another and towards the State can be influenced by Christian understanding of mutual service and shared responsibility;

3.   the extent to which churches and other Christian groups can bring an experience of community to the neighbourhoods where they are at work.

The churches in Birmingham were looking for a role which would complement that of the statutory services and also engage the energies of their lay members. They asked statutory services and voluntary organisations about unmet need in the community and also about the nature of the contribution they might make. They were, in effect, lining up alongside non-church voluntary organisations and making an offer of voluntary community service to the statutory providers. They wanted to know if the offer was welcome (to the statutory services) and what scope there was for voluntary service by their members. This was the point of the first of their questions and they were left in no doubt that their offer was welcome, provided that the nature of the commitment was understood. They were assured that "there are always people whose situation falls outside the scope of any statutory provision or who require additional care such as a relative or personal friend would normally give". There was plenty of scope for offering the "type of help which can be given directly by one individual to another individual or family, help such as a kindly neighbour would give if one were available". The statutory services would welcome any agency able to recruit volunteers for roles which they – the statutory services – would determine, though the welcome was conditional upon a willingness to commit time in advance and to accept the need for training if it was thought necessary.

The dominant note in the report's elaboration of its concern with elderly people is the elderly in need. This does not mean that all older people are seen as actual or potential recipients of social welfare provision. It is rather that they are concerned principally with those older people who, by virtue of being housebound or disabled or infirm, are likely to benefit from the kind of social welfare activities that the churches might usefully undertake to provide. Some of these people would be members of their own congregations, but only a minority. The report looks to translate into practice, properly organised and coordinated at the appropriate level, a sense of social responsibility which is restricted neither to the family of kin nor to the 'family of the church'. They are committing themselves to work with the same criteria for the assessment of need as those used by the statutory authorities.

The most important factor in determining the nature of the churches' potential contribution to social welfare was the perception shared by statutory services, churches and social researchers of a need for *neighbourliness*. It was the lack of neighbourly concern and friendly contact in new communities, or at any rate communities where people seemed to pass through rather than sink roots, that argued the need for some kind of formal organisation to take over the role of informal networks of neighbourhood care. From this point of view two questions might be asked of the churches. Could they provide the voluntary help that would substitute for the neighbourly helping hand? And could they help to regenerate the more spontaneous informal networks whose absence was regretted by statutory services and churches alike? There were, in other words, two distinct roles which the churches might fill. The first role they could and did share with other non-church voluntary agencies: a source of voluntary help to be drawn on by the statutory services. It seems to have been the view, or the hope, of the Birmingham Social Responsibility Project that the second role was one which the churches were specially (perhaps uniquely) fitted to fill.

There are plenty of examples from the 1950s and 1960s of voluntary care organisations which had clearly identifiable Christian origins and which acted independently of the statutory services as experiments in social care (for example, The Samaritans). The Birmingham project, on the other hand, looked to develop a form of *partnership* with the statutory services at neighbourhood level, acknowledging that the statutory services should take the lead in setting the terms of co-operation. And it was not long after the Birmingham Project that central government put its full weight behind the promotion of what became known as good neighbour schemes. By providing "voluntary co-operation and help at street level" these schemes responded to "the lack of meaningful relationships with others in the modern urban neighbourhood [which] leaves many people friendless, isolated and deprived of neighbourly help in time of crisis" (NCSS 1968). By the late 1960s the regeneration of neighbourliness had become a widely shared goal among makers of social policy. Good Neighbour schemes had sprung up all over the country some of them managed by churches, but many in the hands of secular organisations.

Among the various schemes established in the 1960s which took their inspiration from the Birmingham project were the Fish Scheme in Banbury and the work undertaken by the Churches' Council for Community Care in Sheffield. The Fish Scheme was one of the first church-sponsored neighbourhood schemes. The town was divided into areas each in turn sub-divided into streets with volunteer wardens. People who wanted to make use of the scheme were asked to display a special card in their window; and wardens made regular checks of their streets to see whether the cards were being displayed. All households had been circulated with information on how the scheme worked and had been told that members of the scheme would be willing to assist with matters such as "transport difficulties to hospital, visiting, shopping, and gardening". According to the organisers, older people were the biggest users of the scheme (Lowe 1969). Fish Schemes subsequently spread to many other parts of the country.

The Churches' Council for Community Care (CCCC) in Sheffield, set up in 1966 (and still in existence), was a complex alliance between religious welfare agencies and the statutory authorities for the purpose of "coordinating and supporting neighbourhood care and Good Neighbouring" in the city (Abrams et al 1981). Most of the schemes working in the city in the 1970s belonged to this network; no non-Christian denominations were involved. Three different kinds of venture operated under the aegis of the CCCC: Good Neighbourhood Liaison Schemes; the Community Care Volunteers project; and Good Neighbour "Contact" Schemes. The Good Neighbourhood Liaison Schemes worked through unpaid Liaison Officers appointed by the Churches' Council with responsibility for a specified area, within which he or she would be "prepared to receive calls for help from statutory workers, hospitals, doctors, clergy, domiciliary services and other organisations (i.e. referrals), and then to find suitable local helpers to take on the necessary work". The Community Care Volunteers project was launched partly to meet the need for long-term visiting and specialised help which was seen to be beyond the capacity of the Liaison Schemes. The most recent of the ventures, the Contact Scheme, was "directed towards the ordinary residents of Sheffield rather than the array of service-providing agencies ... but whereas the Liaison Scheme is designed to help clients 'found' by the medical and social services, the Contact Scheme depends on the direct monitoring of need among neighbours". The contacts were "people willing to keep their eyes open on a few houses in their neighbourhood for any signs of emergency ... so that anyone in difficulty has someone near at hand who is touch with the people who can help" (Abrams et al 1981).

An example of a much smaller scheme is provided by the Bradbury Christian Council project set up in 1977.

> With advice from the Social Services Department, it was decided that a Visiting service for the elderly and housebound would be initiated. Social Services were asked to provide the names of people in the area who could benefit from such a service.... The scheme has provided a consistent and continuing visiting service on a small scale. (Bulmer 1986)

The Bradbury Project exemplifies a pattern noted by Abrams and colleagues in their 1981 review of Good Neighbour Schemes: the vast majority of UK schemes were engaged in home-visiting and the elderly were their core client group.

What the Banbury, Sheffield and Bradbury schemes have in common is that they were launched by local churches, who provided the "formal framework for the cultivation of informality". And as Abrams points out, "by far the most common source of [Good Neighbour] schemes is organised Christianity". Thirty-nine per cent of the 1,000 schemes reviewed by the Volunteer Centre had been initiated by churches, 27% by voluntary organisations, 16% by local residents and 13% by local authorities or parish councils. Furthermore 60% of the church-initiated schemes had been in existence for more than five years – a figure that contrasts dramatically with the 65% of social-service initiated schemes that had come into being within the previous five years. The finding was indeed somewhat unexpected. "What we find remarkable is that the churches should play such an important role in a society where, on the one hand, religious observance seems to have suffered a drastic decline and where, on the other, efforts have been made by successive governments to foster organised neighbourliness on a strictly secular basis" (Abrams et al 1981). Even when the churches had no such organisational role to play, their support was often vital for the running of the schemes. "About 60% of Good Neighbour Schemes could equally well be described as Good Christian schemes and across the whole range of informal caring, from nursing dependent relatives at home to visiting and doing odd jobs for strangers, people with a strong sense of religious commitment are disproportionately active" (Abrams 1985).

Not all local churches participated in Good Neighbour Schemes, however, and even when they did, the size of their contribution to informal care in the neighbourhood should be set in its proper context. As Abrams (1985) points out, about 90% of the care given to those who cannot fend for themselves in our society is given by spouses, children and other kin. For many churches their contribution to informal care in the neighbourhood would probably have corresponded to that made by what Hornsby-Smith (1989) thinks of as the typical Catholic parish:

> Tentatively it is suggested that *personal* and *domestic* care, where provided, are substantially given by close family members, particularly daughters, and there is very little provision of this type of care by parishioners. Some *auxiliary* care [i.e. shopping, transport etc] may be offered either on an intermittent and less frequently a sustained basis, particularly for the elderly and the housebound. This might, in a post-Vatican II parish with a well-developed sense of the value of lay ministries, be linked to the regular distribution of Communion by a team of special ministers. Occasionally senior children from a local secondary school will be involved in intermittent help, particularly shopping for the housebound. Parishioner care, where it is at all developed, is most likely to be found in the provision of *social* support [i.e. informal counselling and emotional support].

The argument advanced by Abrams in 1985 that any policy for informal care should begin with the "problems and possibilities of supporting the bonds of kinship" is now quite widely accepted of course. That the churches were not behindhand in recognising the importance of the family as a source of informal care to older people as well as the strains that the provision of informal care may impose on family life can be seen, for example, in the recent report from the Church of England report (1995) on the family.

BEYOND WELFARISM

The report of the Birmingham Social Responsibility Project represents the 'first thoughts' of the churches in post-war Britain about the nature of their changing responsibilities towards older members of the community. Subsequent reports from church bodies have tended to develop themes which call into question the 'welfarist' or 'service-oriented' approach to social concern adopted in the Birmingham study: the desire to find a distinctive role for the church, a role which would distinguish them from non-church voluntary organisations; a renewed emphasis on loneliness as a cause of unhappiness in the lives of older people; the reaction against community *service* in favour of community *development*; and the promotion of a positive view of ageing.

In the 1960s, one of the main sources of scepticism about the Birmingham 'model' appears to have been concern about the distinctive role of the churches in society. Certainly not all the churches, or at any rate not all of their paid clergy, welcomed the proposal for a partnership with the statutory services. The 1962 Buckingham survey of clergy suggests that the majority of clergy in this prosperous and largely rural county saw the development of secular institutions of social welfare not as a challenge but as a liberation. It would allow them "to concentrate their undivided attention upon the spiritual welfare of their parishioners", which included "giving spiritual help to those faced with grave personal difficulties". This is not to deny that "members of the church should play a [larger] part in alleviating the loneliness of housebound people". There is, however, a difference between encouraging a sense of social responsibility among individual members of a congregation and developing a partnership with social services to promote the welfare of the *whole* community. The church *as an institution* should not lose sight of its distinctive role in society.

Criticism of the way in which the churches have exercised their responsibilities for the *spiritual* well-being of their older members is a recurrent theme in the more recent religious literature on ageing. To cite only one example, a recent working party report from the dioceses of Rochester and Canterbury (1992) conceded that "clergy were sometimes more willing to offer a careful ministry of preaching, teaching and pastoral care to young people than old". Assumptions could be made too easily "about an older person's spiritual maturity, and about where they are on their spiritual journey.... Yet it is often at this time in a person's life that spiritual concerns assume a greater significance and spiritual needs a greater urgency. Evangelism among older people may be more about sitting and listening, than about proclaiming." The institutions of organised religion are urged to develop "appropriate forms of evangelism among older people", and clergy should "recognise that the spiritual needs and concerns of older people have a legitimate claim on their time and resources".

It was indeed out of a sense of precisely these kinds of shortcomings in the Christian churches that the ecumenical Christian Council on Ageing (CCOA) was established ten years earlier in 1982: "to explore the Christian potential and vocation in later years and nurture the continuing development of faith and growth; to affirm the contribution of local people to their local church and community; to improve the pastoral care of elderly people, and their opportunities for worship and fellowship."

It was the same question of the distinctive role of the churches as religious institutions that exercised a working party of clerical and lay people convened in 1968 by the National Old People's Welfare Council (NOPWC) to consider the role of the churches in the care of the elderly. The members of this working party shared a concern that

> in the developing picture of the social services, there may be a lack of coordination between religious groups and a danger of overlapping in the services provided. It has further been suggested that the professed follower of any faith has a unique part to play and that this might be lost sight of in the picture of total care if there were pressure on religious bodies to develop the kind of welfare services that could, and are, being carried out by secular bodies.

The working party argued that "the churches, the clergy and the laity, have a specific service to offer in the total welfare of old people". The churches should take up the challenge of defining the specific nature of their contribution to the welfare of older people and "suggest ways in which the specific, distinctive role of the churches may become increasingly effective". They wondered if Good Neighbourhood Schemes lacked something which was part of 'true' neighbourliness. Did they foster *"mutual* relationships in which joys and sorrows, the everyday happenings of life, are shared as well as the occasional emergency"?

What concerned the NOPWC working party was the *personal* side of the problem of social isolation – the experience of loneliness – the same problem highlighted by Seebohm Rowntree in the late 1940s in his discussion of the need for companionship. Although social isolation is recognised as a root problem in the Birmingham report and the importance of friendly contacts and the making of personal relationships is emphasised again and again, the problem of loneliness stands in the background rather than the foreground of the report. Its main interest is the potential contribution of volunteers and neighbours to practical social care. On the one hand, there are people in need of care and support, and on the other hand, there are people who are willing to do things *for* them – to provide a helping hand, and give practical help in the business of everyday life. The relationship of social worker (or the volunteer as auxiliary social worker) to client is of course different from that of neighbour to neighbour.

It was, as already mentioned, one of the aims of the Birmingham project, to build up a sense of community which would lead to spontaneous offers of help between neighbours – offers made, in other words, on the basis of the sort of friendly relations that characterise good neighbours. Neighbourliness, in this context, is seen as an instrumental good; it is the expression of a sense of mutual obligation among members of a community; and sustains networks of informal care. What the NOPWC working party wishes to see is something different from this: a kind of neighbourliness which is valued not (or not only) as a source of mutual aid but as an expression of 'human togetherness'. And they are critical of the type of voluntary action in which the churches had become involved in the 1960s because it tended to foster one aspect of neighbourliness but not the other.

For several church-based reports or publications looking specifically at the welfare of older people in the community, loneliness is highlighted as an important common problem in later life. In 1969, for example, a survey of the *Churches' role in the care of the elderly in Banbury*, acknowledging the continuing presence of physical suffering in the elderly (caused by poverty and sometimes also by a "stubborn independence amongst the old"), was struck by the fact that

> the attention of those concerned with the welfare of the old is now increasingly being placed upon the mental suffering involved in growing old. The departure of children from the home, retirement, widowhood, the depression caused by the decline of physical and mental faculties, and perhaps most important of all the loneliness that is a natural concomitant to all the former are facets of this mental anguish which is so commonplace but so rarely answered adequately by the community. (Lowe 1969)

A more tentative approach to the problem of loneliness in later life is taken in an earlier report by the Maidstone Council of Churches (1965), following a survey which attempted to assess local need in "a prosperous county town". Although the report concluded that loneliness was one of the major ills of modern society, it was recognised as a problem that may afflict young as well as old, which, of course, is not to say that it is not a major problem among older people. "Many elderly people lead empty lives, having hardly any contact with the outside world and no one to whom they can turn in times of illness or worry."

The theme is picked up once again in a 1980 report of a working party set up by Age Concern England to study the role of religious organisations in the welfare of the elderly. Following in the footsteps of the 1968 NOPWC discussion paper, though with a clearer sense of the source of their dissatisfaction, the report from the 1980 working party asserts that "today there are new needs which cannot be satisfied merely by a 'welfare' approach". And prominent among these is loneliness.

> Over a million elderly people are living alone. A survey among those aged 75 or more discovered that 20 per cent feel acutely lonely.... The same survey found that 35 per cent of those living alone "never dreamed that they could be so lonely". This is a new problem in society, exacerbated by smaller families and by increased mobility. All the clubs, day centres and good neighbour schemes, and the profusion of other services, have so far failed to find a solution. (Age Concern 1980)

The Age Concern report is reiterating the view already expressed by the NOPWC in 1968: Good Neighbour schemes have their limitations. The kind of neighbourliness they promote does little to relieve the loneliness experienced by so many older people. This is, of course, not for want of trying. A befriending service was, after all, part and parcel of what most Good Neighbour Schemes saw themselves as offering.

To understand the importance and significance of the problem of loneliness is to recognise the limitations of what the author of a Jubilee Centre report on the care of older people (Burton-Jones 1990) criticises as a "materialistic emphasis" in our understanding of the needs of older people for practical support from the church and community. This is common ground shared by all the various church-based reports which highlight the problem of loneliness. The community's response to the needs of older people living in the community is inadequate if it cannot see beyond the need for practical help with the business of everyday life, i.e. informal (or formal) social care. Where Seebohm Rowntree and Beveridge are quite happy to talk about the need for companionship, the more recent church-based reports look to classify these needs in terms of the framework of ideas used by the churches to discuss the relationship between their own distinctive role in society, their special sphere of competence, and the demonstration of social concern.

Loneliness is cited therefore as an example of a 'spiritual need'. It is furthermore a need which is not restricted to members of religious communities. It is suggested, in other words, that the churches have a distinctive part to play in promoting the welfare of *all* older people in the community (i.e. not only their own members) – a role which distinguishes them from non-church voluntary agencies as well as statutory authorities – insofar as it addresses needs which are their special province. The church should exercise its social responsibility to promote the welfare of older people by meeting the kind of spiritual need that is exemplified in loneliness. Like the 1961 Birmingham report, it is in the existence of unmet need that these later reports find a role for the churches complementary to that of the statutory services. Where they differ from the Birmingham report is in their use of a distinction between what would now be called social care needs, on the one hand, and what are identified as spiritual needs, on the other.

The late 1960s and the 1970s were a time of growing enthusiasm for community development, and the churches were very much affected by this. In 1968 the Gulbenkian Foundation, in its report on community work and social change, was somewhat critical of the churches for trying to cling onto welfare activities which had been largely taken over by the statutory authorities and urged them to explore new areas such as community work. In 1976 the British Council of Churches published a report on community work which argued that the churches had in the past put too much emphasis on community *service* and had neglected their role as agents of social change within the local community, a role in which they would act *with* local people rather than providing something *for* them. The report also recognised, however, that times were changing and that "many Christians, ordained and lay, had recently become deeply committed to various types of community work at parish and neighbourhood level". The period between these two reports coincides, in other words, with a new wave of growth for the voluntary sector beyond a service-providing role (Brenton 1985), and this wave swept the churches along with it.

It seems moreover that the wave gathered force during the 1980s and has maintained its momentum through the 1990s. A 1990 report from the British Council of Churches (Ballard 1990) points to "an upsurge in Christian social concern" during the time of the Thatcher government.

> Above all there are countless scores of local activities from major schemes and large community centres to small projects using the local church hall for self-help groups or play groups. And this obviously transcends traditional theological and ecclesiastical barriers witnessing to a new ecumenism.... Almost every congregation will claim to be doing some community related activity.

The claim is reiterated by the Archbishop of Canterbury, who said in a lecture to the Abbeyfield Society that "we [in the Churches] run a vast number of voluntary projects to assist older people in the community" (Carey 1997).

Although recent published material on the welfare activities of the churches is relatively sparse and patchy, what is available does serve to give some idea of the range of their community-based activities. "The six main black-led churches in Leeds are each planning or running a community project. They have jointly decided on these projects which include ... a workshop for the 50+ age group" (Howard 1987). The Church of England report on *Faith in the countryside* (1990), which takes the view that "Parochial Church Councils ought to be active in considering the well-being of *all* the people in the parish", offers a few examples of activity found in rural dioceses: a 'Circle of Care' in Wiltshire which provides "training of a practical nature for carers"; in Surrey a volunteer drivers scheme; and in Portsmouth and Winchester, diocesan advisers who encourage the establishment of what are in effect good neighbour schemes.

A report from the Centre for Voluntary Organisations at the London School of Economics (Harris 1995) outlines a typology of the welfare activities in four London congregations, and highlights the importance of informal care *within* the network of relationships formed by the congregation itself. In only one of the congregations, a black Pentecostal church, was there an organised welfare project dedicated to older people, and that was a day care centre. Chester and Smith (1996), like Harris, emphasise the importance of "informal networks of caring" in their study of four London congregations. The provision of day care is also the subject of a recent study of the important role played by the Scottish churches in the provision of community-based services for people with dementia (Murphy 1997). What enables the churches to play this role is the availability of buildings for community use.

The authors of the Birmingham report, as we have already seen, hoped that, as well as providing volunteers for community services, the churches might also help to mobilise energies and resources in the wider local community for what Abrams subsequently called the project of neighbourhood care. Furthermore it was in this second role, in promoting the development of a sense of shared responsibility in the wider community, that they thought to find a distinctive role for the churches. In the event, however, it seems that many of the church-based neighbourhood projects which were inspired by the Birmingham scheme were essentially ways of coordinating voluntary community service, encouraged by statutory providers who recognised that the churches had an important role to play in encouraging the altruism that helped sustain voluntary informal care. Was it perhaps that the Birmingham churches were rather naive in thinking that the goals of 'community development' might be achieved as a kind of spin-off from a community service project? However this may be, the churches do seem to have shown a growing preference in recent years for the ideals and goals of community development and for a more direct approach to 'community-building'. A preference which is indicative of the efforts they have made to shed the image of "philanthropy and churchy bourgeois attitudes" so inimical to Crossman and his colleagues. Witness *Faith in the city*.

> We have made our recommendations about the pattern of Church life which we believe should emerge within urban priority areas, and have emphasised the need for a commitment to neighbourliness and community. We see community work as a legitimate lay ministry.

Community development goes in hand in hand with 'empowerment'. As a general rule it is better to empower older people to do things for themselves than to do things for them. This does not mean that the 'old' idea of community service is jettisoned. What it does mean, however, is that the churches should reconsider the channels through which they express social concern for older people. The importance of the idea of empowerment can be clearly seen in the report of the south Yorkshire-based Faith in Elderly People Project (1991). Churches in the area were urged to "identify some examples of older people's power being used effectively, or some local self-help schemes" and ask themselves how they might "work alongside groups of elderly people in order to encourage them to recognise their unique value and to organise together to combat ageism". They should also "urge the establishment locally of an Elderly People's Forum, so that older people can speak for themselves, especially during the planning of the new community care arrangements". The view of the religious community as a resource (composed of active and committed individuals) which can be mobilised to improve the welfare of older people (those in need) should be corrected by recognising that older people themselves constitute a resource which is too often under-valued and under-developed. As Chester and Smith (1996) point out, the contribution of older members of religious congregations is often considerable.

Although the idea of empowerment does not altogether undermine the 'call' for community service, it leads inevitably to a change in priorities. In place of an emphasis on the churches as sources of community volunteers and potential providers of neighbourhood care, there is an emphasis on the importance of the informal care provided by the family. The churches seem to have come round to the view that they would do better to put their energies into supporting family carers than into developing the project of neighbourhood care. It is interesting in this connection to note the reservations of the Canterbury and Rochester working party on ageing (see above) about volunteering.

> A word of warning is in order. Church congregations tend to contain a higher-than-average proportion of elderly people. They also include lay people whose work is fully stretching and is itself the proper place of their ministry. It is important therefore to assess how much pastoral care members of a congregations can be asked to offer. In particular, suppositions that the local church can pick up care previously offered by statutory bodies may not be realistic.

Throughout the 1960s and 1970s social policy debate about the position of older people was dominated by the concept of need. What did older people need by way of services, support and help? What role should the churches play in meeting these needs? In the 1980s and 1990s the churches saw, with increasing clarity, that an another kind of response was required of them. What was required was not simply the criticism of public policy but the denunciation of prevailing values. Alongside the various manifestations of the social neglect of older people, there is another problem, the devaluation of old age, which goes hand-in-hand with the idolisation of youth. In 1979, in an article entitled *The spiritual neglect of the elderly*, the Bishop of Southwell highlights loss of dignity as "one of the great deprivations that old people suffer nowadays".

> This loss of dignity which comes from our tendency to declare redundant our maturer members of society is one of the most hurtful aspects of modern life. (Wakeling 1979)

The devaluation of old age is the first and most prominent of the various needs highlighted by the 1980 Age Concern report as examples of new needs which cannot be satisfied merely by a welfare approach.

> Contemporary society imposes second class status upon many of its older members. It does so by shunting them from the main line on to the sidings, but also by the values it adopts. Experience is the special possession of elderly people, as is the wisdom which it nurtures but, in a period of change, people feel that experience is of little value. Youth is the time of life which is valued and applauded.

The Irish Council of Churches (ICC) (1989), an ecumenical body in Northern Ireland, makes the same point when it puts at the head of its list of the "needs of the elderly", the "need to have a recognised place in the community". What are the churches to do about the increasing prominence of values which they deplore? They should speak out; they should adopt what the working party calls a 'prophetic stance'.

> We believe that society needs to hear the religious voice, stating unchanging principles and encouraging our changing world to think again about its attitude to older people; to respect them as fully responsible adults and to recognise the inhumanity of much that it allows or fosters today.

In 1990 the Board of Social Responsibility of the Church of England published its report on *Ageing*. The most substantial of all the official post-war Church reports on this topic, its very title strikes a different note from most of those which preceded it. It is concerned, not with a sub-group of the population, but with a process which now affects almost everyone. Like the ICC report published one year earlier, its central theme is the 'new' view of ageing associated with the idea of Third Age and the emergence of social gerontology as a distinct academic discipline. The element in the social situation which calls for a response from the churches is not the inadequacy of the welfare state to meet the needs of the older population; it is rather the inadequacy of the ideas of human ageing that shape both individual attitudes and institutional policy, within the churches and outside them.

In 1961 the position of older people in the community engaged the interest of the churches as one of many needy groups within the community. The churches were reassessing their social responsibilities in the light of the developing institutions of the welfare state and asked themselves how they might mobilise their resources to promote the welfare of the housebound elderly – to help meet the needs of individuals who could not fend for themselves. In 1990 the position of older people engaged the interest of the Church of England because that position was itself subject to revaluation. The responsibility of the Church for the welfare of the older population as a whole is to be exercised not by mobilising resources to meet needs but through "critical and theological reflection" on the ideas that shape policy. It is no longer the existence of unmet need which determines the response of the church to the question: how should we exercise our social responsibilities? The Church does not see itself as 'in the business' of offering a service-based response to the problem of unmet need in the elderly population as a whole. Or rather it wishes to discard formulations of its role which place too much emphasis on doing things *for* older people.

No doubt there are various reasons for the change of emphasis noted in the Church of England report prominent among which, as I have already suggested, is the growing influence and recognition of 'new ideas'. What is also of importance, however, is the fact that this is a single denomination report. Most of the earlier reports we have cited have an ecumenical stance. They ask, what should *we* the churches do about this? They look for common ground as a basis for *collective* action. They take for granted their responsibilities for their own elderly members and ask about the nature of their wider responsibilities. If the Church of England draws back from this stance, it is presumably not because of an aversion to ecumenism, but because of uncertainty about the nature of its responsibilities to help meet unmet need in the community as a whole, and also because it wishes to take a critical look at its responsibilities to its own members.

In the light of 'new ideas', and above all the 'new idea' of ageism, how should the Church exercise its responsibilities towards its older members? What guides the Church in its deliberations on this question is the idea of fairness or justice. It wants to ensure that older people are not denied their rightful place within the 'community of believers' and asks about the rights and duties which define this place. The integrity of the religious community should be maintained even when physical and mental decline threaten to sever the links between the individual and that community.

CONCLUSION

This chapter has looked at what the Christian churches have had to say, in the last fifty years or so, about the position of older people in Britain and also about what they owe to older people in consequence of this position. And despite the historical approach, the preceding pages should not be read as a history, let alone a contemporary description, of the welfare *activities* of British churches in this field. Primary sources of information have been neglected in favour of a handful of official and semi-official reports, together with a few surveys – and there are indeed not many – which consider the kinds of practical response demanded from the churches by the position of older people ('demanded' because they are by self-definition caring communities). The central question for these reports has been, what is to be done? As we have seen, their answers have varied along with their understanding of the situation about which something is to be done. Most of them have looked to identify appropriate channels for the expression of social concern which complement the work of statutory social welfare agencies and harmonise with their conception of the 'proper part' to be played in society by the churches as religious institutions and as religious communities within a wider community. They have asked how the churches should discharge their responsibilities towards older people *inside and outside of* the churches without losing sight of their distinctive role, and their insistence on values which "lie beyond the satisfaction of mere material needs" (*Faith in the city*). Their answers have tended to make wide use of the language of community in a form which emphasises the full participation by individual members of the community in the exercise of these responsibilities, rather than the delegation of these responsibilities to a specialist agency which exercises them on their behalf.

The lack of published secondary material on the welfare activities of the churches makes it difficult to paint a fair and accurate picture of the contribution made by religious groups to the social welfare of older people. How do their efforts compare with, and how do they fit in with, the network of age-specialised secular voluntary organisations which has grown so rapidly in recent years? Has there been a shift away from projects which coordinate the efforts of community service volunteers to other types of activity such as the provision of day centres? How effective are different religious communities as sources of mutual aid and social support to their own older members and also as vehicles for a certain kind of community development – for extending community-like interaction and informal care to other people in need in the same locality? What balance do they strike between the expression of social concern and the performance of distinctively spiritual functions? It would be very difficult to answer these questions and get a good picture of what is being done by the churches today without primary research. Certainly the argument developed in the preceding pages – that the last twenty years or so have seen increasing scepticism about the appropriateness of 'welfarist' models for the expression of social concern towards older people – should not be taken to imply that the churches have abandoned those activities to which they attached such importance in the 1960s. Increasingly, however, they have had to recognise that they are themselves 'fragile communities' and in these circumstances the tension between their sense of responsibility to their own members and an ideal of service to the whole community can only become more acute.

3
RELIGION, SPIRITUALITY
AND WELL-BEING

The meaning of life is to be found solely in man's relationship to God. It is this relationship which gives meaning to all human values. In the light of it, every period of life, including that of old age, is possessed of intrinsic value and sublime potential. Viewed in the light of an eternal destiny, old age is seen to have an importance as great as that of youth or the middle years. To young and old, the divine imperative is addressed: "Thou shalt love the Lord thy God ... and thy neighbour as thyself."

In 1961 the White House Conference on Aging (WHCA) met "to consider and propose solutions for the problems and dislocations created for individuals, families, communities, and society by the suddenness with which the older population had increased". The conference devoted most of its attention to a multitude of issues to do with service provision and financial support, arguments about distributive justice, about the steps that should be taken to ensure that older people receive their fair share of basic social goods and services.

The report of the Religion and Aging Section of the conference, which opens with the resounding and unabashedly religious affirmation of equality cited at the head of this chapter, insists, however, that the issues raised by the advent of an ageing society extend beyond problems of distributive justice. The authors are concerned in particular with the prevailing values of American society, especially its tendency towards "the glorification of youth and the denigration of old age". They analyse the situation in terms which were hardly a novelty even then. Social and economic change had transformed old age into a 'roleless role'; and demographic change ensured that the role was occupied, with varying degrees of reluctance, by increasing numbers of older people. The plight of the elderly was tied up with the fact that society had developed in such a way that it no longer had any use for older people.

The diagnosis would be familiar to many of the other participants of the WHCA. What gives the Religion and Ageing report its distinctive stamp is the scepticism it displays towards proposals to solve the problem simply by removing barriers that stand in the way of older people's participation in the social worlds of work and leisure. This may be part of the answer, but it is not the whole of it. "The

59

goal is *not* to keep the aging busy." The problem, they think, lies deeper than that, and reflects the community's loss of any shared sense of the meaningfulness of life apart from the production and consumption of wealth. It is for this reason that they give such prominence to the beliefs of the Jewish and Christian religions about the eternal destiny of the human individual as a source of the intrinsic value of human life. Their claim that "religion, in its teaching, ritual and organization, is uniquely equipped to guide and aid men in making the closing years of life a time of deepening fulfilment" is grounded in the conviction that well-being in later life depends on more than the provision of goods and services, or the development of opportunities for work and leisure. Secular institutions concerned with developing and implementing society's collective response to the problems of an ageing society are therefore urged to take note of the place claimed by religion in human life and the nature of its contribution to well-being in later life.

For policy makers and social researchers who do not share its avowedly religious viewpoint, the interest of the report of the Religion and Aging section of the WHCA hinges on the claim that religion has an important and possibly distinctive contribution to make to well-being in later life. The claim was no doubt intended as a challenge, both to the institutions of organised religion (to 'get their act together') and to secular institutions concerned with promoting the well-being of older people. Much of what has been written on religion and ageing since the early 1960s takes up this same challenge, sometimes explaining the connection between religion and successful ageing from a position of explicit religious conviction, sometimes investigating the connection from a position of scientific detachment.

Ministers of religion and theologians who ask about well-being in later life are of course engaged in a somewhat different task from gerontologists who ask about religion's contribution to well-being in later life. It is part and parcel for those with religious conviction that the tradition to which they belong has something to offer older people, as it has something to offer everybody. To say what the benefits are or how they relate to a particular time of life is a task of theological interpretation, not empirical enquiry. Social scientists look at the matter in quite a different way. They are interested only in those benefits that can be discerned by empirical methods and explained by testable theories.

Despite these differences, however, their approaches are not completely divergent. Certainly the scientific literature on ageing is of interest to clergy and theologians who write about ageing. They want to assess the implications of this literature for their own profession or discipline. They feel bound to "address the mounting research on aging" (Bianchi 1982). They also hope, and this is the important point, that the traffic in ideas will not be one-way.

> I will be proposing a theological interpretation of aging. I will be suggesting that the Christian community has something important to say, grounded in its own identity as a community, both to itself and to the wider world about the meaning of human fulfilment in aging. (Lyon 1985)

It is beyond the compass of this report to consider such theological interpretations (Christian or non-Christian) of ageing in any depth or detail. They are part of the province of theology. What does not belong to theology is the claim that these ideas are of relevance to a wider debate about ageing and the position of older people. By the same token, it is beyond the compass of this report to offer a detailed assessment of the social science research into the connection between religion and successful ageing. To ask, however, whether or not the research has any practical implications outside the institutions of organised religion is a question about public policy. These two issues, which together represent the convergence of two quite different viewpoints on one and the same topic, provide the framework for this chapter.

THE RELIGIOUS STANDPOINT

The report of the Religion and Aging Section of the 1961 WHCA is one of the earliest contributions to what has since become a steady stream of policy documents about older people or ageing which issue from various churches and inter-denominational committees. Many of these reports are concerned first and foremost with the policy and practice of the particular religious organisations and communities to which their authors belong, though many of them, like the White House Conference policy statement, also have something to say, or believe that they have something to say, to everyone "who shares their concern for the aged". The reports of the Church of England's Board of Social Responsibility and the Irish Council of Churches raise issues and sound themes which had occupied the attention of their American colleagues for nearly thirty years.

Alongside all these official and semi-official reports, there is a large and growing body of literature which is also firmly grounded in a religious viewpoint, but concentrates on personal rather than collective responses to the phenomenon of ageing. These are books and papers which lay the foundations for many of the policy recommendations found in the official reports by asking whether and how a religious standpoint should influence the way in which individuals respond to the changes that accompany the onset of late life.

In the late 1960s the SCM (Student Christian Movement) Press invited the Swiss doctor and psychotherapist, Paul Tournier, to write a book about the problems of retirement from work. *Learning to grow old* (1972) was conceived partly as a work of spiritual counsel and guidance, something that older people themselves might find useful, and partly also as an aid to ministers of religion who might be called on to provide spiritual counsel and guidance as part of their pastoral responsibilities. What calls for counsel and guidance in this case is a kind of crisis or problem that may afflict non-believers quite as much as believers. It is not, in other words, a problem which can only arise for those who are committed to a certain religious standpoint, like a crisis of faith or certain kinds of moral dilemma. It is rather a common human experience like marital discord or bereavement. Tournier sees his role, or the pastoral role, in all this as an extension of his therapeutic role. It is less a matter of helping people resolve their uncertainties about what to do or what to think than of helping them see through what is often a very distressing experience, namely, growing old.

For his starting point Tournier takes up what he calls the Jungian view that "it is impossible to live through the evening of life in accordance with the programmes appropriate to the morning, since what had great importance then will have very little now, and the truth of the morning will be the error of the evening" (Jung 1933).There are, in fact,

> two great turning points in life: the passage from childhood to adulthood and that from adulthood to old age ... and we measure our success in negotiating the first, Freudian, turning point – becoming adult – in terms of our success in love and in our career. Later on, the success we make of our retirement will be the test of our success in negotiating the second, Jungian, turning point – the maturity of the person.

The aim then is to help people make the passage from adulthood to old age, and more particularly to consider how the Christian faith might make a difference to the way in which we negotiate this second great turning point in life. The significance of *Learning to grow old* is that it is one of the first of many books and articles, most of them published in the USA, which ask about the influence of a particular religious standpoint on personal responses to ageing.

It is essential to Tournier's understanding of the stage of life with which he is concerned – old age – that its problems and difficulties are not simply a product of social relations which are in principle amenable to modification by collective effort.

Among the ills of the aged, there are some that come from men, from their prejudices, from their lack of love, from their contempt, from the way society is organised and its inequity.... But there are others which come from Nature, and fighting against the laws of Nature only brings fresh suffering.... Who can deny that being born, growing, maturing, declining and dying – that all this is a part of Nature?

We are to distinguish between collective effort to change the social position of older people and the personal task of learning to grow old. The personal task, argues Tournier, is inescapable, except for those who die early, and it may be done well or badly. What is required, above all else, for the successful prosecution of this task is what Tournier calls acceptance, a notion which he is at some pains to distinguish from fatalistic resignation or stoical fortitude. He claims to share Simone de Beauvoir's (1972) distaste for the moralist who preaches a gospel of endurance and emphasises that he is trying to help with "the removal of obstacles to the harmonious evolution of life". "To accept is to assent freely to what life demands." What is it that is so difficult to accept in old age? It is this: "how can the person who has seen a meaning in life also see a meaning in old age, which seems to him to be a diminution, an amputation, a stifling of life?"

Seven years later, quarrying in the same vein, Catholic theologian Charles Curran (1981) wrote that

> The challenge of old age is to be truly active – in the sense of accepting old age, appropriating it, giving it meaning, and integrating it into oneself as a person. Some philosophers characterize the human person as a meaning-giver. This is the active aspect of personal development for all of us – to give meaning to our existence and to incorporate all the realities of life into the integrated whole of the person. Yes, in a technological sense we produce less in old age; we do less in the terms of the material and the physical; but we are called upon to be active, to give meaning and intelligibility to our lives. The old and the old-old should truly be active in the most personal sense of being active – giving meaning and intelligibility to their lives.

Where Tournier is practical and offers spiritual counsel and guidance, Curran is reflective and expounds the ideas which should underlie and inform such counsel and guidance. A more recent example of the former genre is *Winter grace: spirituality for the later years* by Kathleen Fischer (1985), who senses a new enthusiasm for her topic.

> Although studies of aging have expanded dramatically during the last few decades, few have taken a spiritual view. Consequently, individuals often fear aging as a downhill battle, a gradual decrease in vitality and increase in vulnerability. The

growing edge of discussion on the meaning of aging is its spiritual dimension.

What stands out in this quotation is the introduction of the idea of the spiritual view. The spiritual life, says Fischer, is not to be equated with churchgoing and religious devotions, and although her own explanation of what it is rather than what it is not is not perhaps very helpful ("By spirituality is meant, not one compartment of life, but the deepest dimension of all life"), the general drift of her meaning is reasonably clear. We think of human powers and capabilities as following a parabolic trajectory through the life course: eventually they stop climbing upwards and take a downward turn. If there is a dimension of life which stands apart from this pattern of change, it is the spiritual dimension. It is here, if anywhere, that we are able to dissociate growing old from loss and decline, which is why Fischer declares that the spiritual dimension of ageing is exciting so much interest amongst gerontologists. The variables which gerontologists typically use to track the ageing of the human organism (variables that measure health status and powers of body and mind) are only part of the story: take a more rounded view of what it means to be human and you will see that real personal growth is possible.

The same metaphor of growth guides K. Brynolf Lyon in *Toward a practical theology of aging* (1985). Lyon, whose aim is to "explore foundational issues in pastoral care with older adults", argues that "there are as many different strands in the understanding of old age in the [Christian] theological tradition as there are in the understanding of anything else in that tradition". There is, however, an underlying image which preserves the unity of the tradition, namely growth. Fulfilment in later life depends on growth; and it is for the theologian to explain what it means, and how it is possible, for the human person to grow in what is also and evidently a time of loss and declining powers. For Lyon it is not enough to say that an older person may grow in spirit even though they weaken and decline in the body. He seeks to explain the idea in terms that would make sense to someone who did not share his religious viewpoint. Growth is possible, he says, through "meeting the developmental challenges that frequently contextualise the diversity of the experience of aging", and the challenges in which he is interested are "those internal and external threats to the meaningfulness of the individual's moral formation that arise with aging".

The religious writings cited in this section bear a family resemblance to works which offer (and discuss) spiritual counsel and guidance on dying and bereavement. They are about more than that final phase of life which is dying, however, and want to determine the boundaries of their topic in some other way than by reference to the process which ends in the final dissolution of the human person. This indeed is what makes them a distinct species within the genus to which they belong, and incidentally makes them interesting to the gerontologist. They claim that there is an inherent unity in their chosen subject matter, something that merits treatment and consideration separately from the problem of facing death. There are obvious common features in the way they conceive of this unity: a common emphasis, for example, on the differences which mark out the burdens and pains of later life from those that afflict people in earlier phases of their lives; a common emphasis also on the inescapability of at least some of these burdens and pains. Most importantly, they are interested in what, from a religious standpoint, appear as the special demands made upon *individuals* by their own ageing, demands which are shaped by the fact that there is something inescapable in the phenomenon of ageing. There is a personal 'task' (like 'calling' the word 'task' is common in writings of this type) to be considered as well as a collective one. All self-conscious human beings are, as it were, called to make something of their lives; it is a fundamental imperative. What are people called to make of their lives when they have put gainful employment and the responsibilities of parenthood behind them or when the problems of what we now call the Fourth Age begin to bite? From the religious standpoint human fulfilment in later life depends on the ability to discern the answer to these questions.

One further characteristic shared by most of the religious works cited in this section is the readiness with which they draw on a tradition of inquiry which takes its bearings mainly from psychoanalysis and psychotherapy for ideas about the critical developmental challenges of later life. Tournier, as we have seen, takes Jung as his guide to the major turning-points in the human life course. Where subsequent theologians and/or pastoral care writers tend to diverge from him is in their account of the nature of these developmental challenges. For the ideas of Jung they have substituted the ideas of later theorists in the same broad tradition, most notably, Victor Frankl (1959) and Erik Erikson (1982). Like Jung, both Frankl and Erikson built their reputations on studies of the developing human personality which take in much more than the transition from childhood to adulthood, arguing that there are other well-defined developmental phases also of critical importance for human well-being.

Like many of those who write about ageing from a religious standpoint, what has characterised much of the work undertaken in this field is an understanding of the phenomenon of ageing which identifies the successful prosecution of a peculiar kind of personal task as a condition of human fulfilment in later life. There is, in short, much common ground between the theologian who understands the work of old age in terms of a transcendent goal and the theorist who wants to talk about existential crises in later life – crises of meaning – and the 'growth' or 'maturity' that comes from facing up to them. What this gives the theologian or pastoral care writer is an opportunity to develop an account of human fulfilment in later life which marries an understanding of ageing from within a religious standpoint with a certain kind of scientific understanding of ageing. Don Browning's *Generative man* (1973) and *Aging as a spiritual journey* by Eugene Bianchi (1982), like Lyon's *Toward a practical theology of ageing*, are all of them examples of attempts to develop an account of human fulfilment in later life which crosses the boundaries between theology and psychodynamic theory.

THE STANDPOINT OF THE SOCIAL
AND BEHAVIOURAL SCIENCES

American social and behavioural scientists, unlike their British counterparts, have long shown a lively interest in the claim that "religion, in its teaching, ritual and organization" has an important and distinctive contribution to make to the well-being and fulfilment of older people.

The USA, despite its thoroughly secular constitution, is even now a more religious country than the United Kingdom. The very presence of a Religion and Aging Section in the White House Conference serves as testimony to this (though subsequent conferences had Spirituality and Aging Sections). A higher proportion of the population adhere to the beliefs and practices of organised religion, mostly Christianity. The 1950s and the early 1960s, furthermore, were a time of religious revival (Greeley 1992). Religion occupied a highly visible place in the lives of many Americans. Some commentators have also seen a "resurgence of interest in religious consciousness and spirituality" in the 1980s and 1990s (Payne 1990). Religion was too prominent in the lives of older Americans for social researchers to be able to ignore it.

A second reason for the receptivity of the academic community to the challenge implicit in the WHCA report may be found in the "common assumption of both laypersons and many scholars ... that as people get older they become more religious" (Markides 1983). The idea that old age is a time of disengagement from active participation in society and preparation for death was, and perhaps still is, commonplace; and the very fact that it is commonplace has encouraged its investigation by social and behavioural scientists. It was not only in the guise of commonplace stereotype that the idea presented itself for criticism, however. In the same year as the first of the White House Conferences, disengagement theory made its appearance as the first full-blown theory of ageing within the social and behavioural sciences (Cummings and Henry 1961). It offered an explanation as well as a description of how people behaved in their later years. Disengagement from social life was, in the favoured language of the time, functional; it was the optimal strategy for ageing. Social and behavioural scientists interested in ageing quickly rounded on disengagement theory; and the contrary strategy, dignified with the name of activity theory, has since gained and held the ascendancy. In other words, interest in the part played by religion in the life of older people chimed in very readily with current debates within the social sciences about ageing as a social phenomenon.

The ground contested by disengagement theory and activity theory is the nature of the adaptive strategy most conducive to well-being in later life. Or, as the question is sometimes phrased nowadays, what makes for successful ageing? The question represents gerontology's claim to combine theory and practice, and is so important to the scientific study of ageing that it could stand as a candidate definition of its subject matter. It is, more than anything else, because of the possibility of a connection between religion and successful ageing that the methods of social science have been brought to bear on the part played by religion in later life.

How should the claim of the WHCA report, that "religion, in its teaching, ritual and organization" has an important and distinctive contribution to make to the well-being and fulfilment of older people, be put to the test of empirical investigation? What is probably still the dominant approach to the investigation has been supplied by the quantitative methodology characteristic of much of the social and behavioural sciences. A probability sample of older people (the bigger the better) is surveyed with a view to examining, by statistical means, the relationship between the distribution of a given indicator of successful ageing (alive or dead? healthy or unhealthy? contented or discontented?) and the distribution of a given indicator of 'religiousness' or 'religiosity'. The US journal literature abounds in studies of this kind. As a general rule, the benefits which researchers are looking for – longevity, health, life-satisfaction, morale, self-esteem – are of such a kind that they may be secured by other means besides religion, for example by physical exercise or social support. These are all standard tools in the research kit of social gerontology. In other words, the conception of personal well-being which is deployed in these investigations owes nothing to the religious viewpoint and everything to measures of health status and well-being that belong to the epidemiology of ageing. Whether it is described as greater well-being or more successful ageing, it is conceived and assessed in ways which make no reference to what might be called the 'spiritual' benefits of religion.

Most reviewers (for example, Koenig 1993; Idler 1994; Levin 1997; Sloan et al 1999) agree that much of the work undertaken in this field is relatively unsophisticated and of poor quality, though many will argue that it is getting better. There is a preponderance of exploratory research designs which do very little to help answer the really interesting questions; the only hypothesis they test is that some measure of well-being is positively associated with some measure of religiosity. In other words, little or no light is thrown on either the nature or direction of any causal relationship. Are the findings to be explained by the fact that religious involvement has an effect on health status? Or is it that health status has an effect on the ability and willingness of the individual to participate in organised religion? It is after all far from implausible to suppose that chronic ill-health and disability may diminish *public* participation in organised religion (Idler 1987). Too many studies suffer from inadequate methodological controls: they fail to make allowance for socio-demographic and personality factors that confounds the interpretation of the results (Levin 1987). There has been, furthermore, a tendency to rely too exclusively on public participation in organised religion as an indicator of religiousness, and to suppose that information about a practice like church attendance is adequate to the task of distinguishing people with religion from people with no religion, as well as the task of distinguishing people who are more intensely religious from those who are less intensely so. There are, however, clear signs of increasing methodological sophistication in the field, which has enabled researchers to secure mainstream funding from the prestigious National Institutes of Health and has also led to "a proliferation of excellent publications in top-line aging journals by a growing cadre of researchers" (Levin 1994).

If religion does have benefits which are detectable by standard methods of investigation, it is important to determine how these effects are obtained. In particular, it is important to ask whether the benefits are to be ascribed to religion *per se*, or to the enhanced social integration that comes with membership of a social group like a church. Is there something distinctive about the mechanism by which the benefits of religion are secured, or does it depend on the performance of a social function, which could, in principle, be performed by non-religious organisations? Are the benefits of religion to be ascribed to an expansion of *social* opportunities and resources or to something else, say an outlook or a set of attitudes, which is more closely woven into the fabric of the individual's personal life?

ENGAGING WITH POLICY AND PRACTICE: THE CONTRIBUTION OF RELIGIOUS INVOLVEMENT TO WELL-BEING IN LATER LIFE

What was described in the last section is an investigation, guided mainly by the kind of methodology that allies the social sciences with epidemiology, into the relationship between, on the one hand, a thoroughly secular idea of individual well-being and, on the other, individual participation in organised religion, that is to say, "religion, in its teaching, organization and ritual". Several reviewers (mainly US reviewers looking at mainly US research) have concluded from the research evidence available to them that religious involvement does make a positive contribution to well-being in later life (for example, Koenig 1993; McFadden 1995; Levin 1997). The practice of religion, in other words, has benefits readily discernible by standard methods of empirical investigation. There are reports of positive associations between religion and a wide range of outcomes, including life expectancy (for example, House et al 1982; Kark et al 1996), survival after cardiac surgery (Oxman et al 1995), functional status (Idler and Kasl 1992), hypertension (Levin and Vanderpool 1989), psychological health and adjustment (Morse and Wisocki 1987), life satisfaction (Hunsberger 1985), self-esteem (Krause 1995), and coping with informal care giving (Rabins et al 1990). There is even a randomised controlled trial of the effects of prayer on cardiovascular disease (Byrd 1988).

Much of the evidence, however, is acknowledged to be unreliable, and it would be wrong to give the impression that there is unanimity over the interpretation of these results in the academic community. A review in the *Lancet* (Sloan et al 1999), for example, concluded that the evidence for an association between religion and *health* was "at best weak and inconsistent", and that we should therefore continue to reserve judgement on the facts of the matter. To adjudicate between the more or less sanguine estimates of the evidence for a positive association between religion and well-being is no part of the aim of this report, however. The intention rather is to concentrate on the possible implications, for policy and practice, of claims, based on empirical research, about the benefits of religion in later life.

On the one hand, there is a body of research which suggests that religious involvement has positive effects on various measurable dimensions of personal well-being in later life. On the other hand, there are policy makers and service providers whose efforts are to be judged against the shared goal of promoting well-being in later life. How, if at all, do the research findings engage with policy goals for an ageing society?

To draw out the implications for policy and practice of evidence for the "salutary effects of religion" (McFadden 1995), it is necessary to consider what the empirical research says about the ways in which religious involvement promotes well-being in later life. What kinds of benefit does it confer and by what means are these effects obtained? The research literature suggests that the causal relationship between religion and well-being in later life may be disclosed in any one of three broad effects and, as we shall see, the implications of this relationship for policy and practice depends on the nature of the effect and the means by which it is achieved.

- Religious involvement has a beneficial effect on health status in later life by preventing morbidity.

- Religious involvement has a beneficial effect on health status in later life by ameliorating the condition of people who are already ill.

- Religious involvement has a beneficial effect on well-being in later life independently of any effect on health status.

The distinction between the first two claims is outlined in a lengthy discussion by Levin (1996) of the interpretation that should be put on the observable association between religious involvement in later life and *health status*. If religious involvement does have an effect on health in later life, that effect may be achieved either by preventing morbidity in later life, or by ameliorating the health status of older people who are already ill or disabled. It is his view that there is no evidence for the hypothesis that

> religious involvement promotes healing.... The data suggest that religious involvement is a protective factor in healthy populations and thus apparently acts in a primary preventive fashion [though the size of the effect appears to be fairly small].... The clinical value of simply being religious has not been studied, and its therapeutic efficacy as a specific strategy for curing disease [or aiding recovery?] seems implausible.

McFadden, in her 1995 review of "the effects of religion upon well-being in later life", distinguishes between the evidence for a causal relationship between religion and health status, which, in her opinion, is relatively strong (better for physical health than mental health), and evidence for a causal relationship between religion and life satisfaction or subjective well-being, which is relatively weak. Life satisfaction is McFadden's preferred term for those aspects of personal well-being which may be assessed independently of health status. Life satisfaction in this sense will be measured by looking at the thoughts and feelings people have about the way their lives are going (or have gone or will go).

It is perhaps worth underlining here McFadden's reservations over the quality of the evidence for a causal relationship between religion and life satisfaction. After all, it may seem rather surprising that there is better evidence for an effect on physical health than on mental health or life satisfaction. *If* religion does indeed make a difference to well-being in later life, we might expect the difference to be most apparent in the thoughts and feelings of older people about the way their lives were going. It seems paradoxical that the evidence should point the other way. Does it mean that the explanation of the effects of health has nothing to do with the thoughts and feelings people have about the way their lives are going? Or does it mean that the instruments by which researchers assess health status are more valid and sensitive than those by which they assess life satisfaction and sense of well-being?

However this may be, it is clearly important to have some idea about the factors that are at work in producing the repeatedly observed and positive association between religious involvement and health status. If it is indeed true that the observations cannot be explained away by the operation of selection bias, we may, following Idler (1987), distinguish four broad hypotheses which might explain how it comes about that religious involvement has a beneficial effect on health and/or well-being. The first of these hypotheses – the health behaviour hypothesis – would account for the observed differences in health status between religious and non-religious people by differences in lifestyle. If religious people were less likely, for example, to smoke or drink excessively than non-religious people, would not this suffice to explain why religious involvement appeared to prevent morbidity in later life? Support for the health behaviour hypothesis may be found in the results of studies which compare individuals with different religious affiliations: there is greater health and less morbidity among adherents of behaviourally strict groups such as Mormons and Seventh Day Adventists (Troyer 1988) and fundamentalist Protestants (Dwyer et al 1990) than there is among adherents of other religious groups or unaffiliated individuals.

All three of the other hypotheses discussed by Idler, unlike the health behaviour hypothesis, purport to explain not only health effects but also differences in well-being that are independent of health status. What Idler calls the social cohesiveness hypothesis points to the fact that "religious groups provide access to emotional, cognitive and material support, fostering the individual's perception that he is cared for and esteemed". There are, and this is amply supported by evidence from both ethnographic and sociological studies, considerable social benefits attached to membership of a religious group. Ellison and George (1994), for example, in a large study in the southeastern United States, found that frequent churchgoers when compared with less frequent churchgoers or 'unchurched' people had larger non-kin social networks, benefited "from a wider array of supportive transactions", and had more favourable perceptions of the quality of their social relationships. "Religious institutions", they say, "foster durable and supportive interpersonal relationships." And there is plenty of evidence for the effect of the quality of social (or emotional) support on health and well-being in later life (House et al 1988). Durable and supportive interpersonal relations are doubtless worth having quite apart from any effect on health. Even so, good social support helps people to cope with illness and disability; it may even help to prevent morbidity.

The two other hypotheses which Idler mentions are closely linked and affirm the importance of the beliefs which help people to make sense of their lives (the coherence hypothesis) and also of distressing boundary situations like physical disability and decline (the theodicy hypothesis). Religion may help people to continue to find meaning and value in their lives at a time when losses and diminishments of various kinds threaten to undermine their sense of meaning and value. This indeed is more or less the same point that was made by the religious writers on ageing cited earlier in the chapter. If the supposed benefits of religion are to be ascribed to religion *per se*, these are the hypotheses for which researchers must find confirming evidence.

If religious beliefs do enable people to bear with losses and illness more easily, it is possible that the effect might be seen not only in their sense of well-being (for example, life satisfaction or emotional distress) but even perhaps in their health status. Certainly the view that physical disease may result from emotional distress, with all that this implies for prevention, is becoming increasingly acceptable to mainstream medicine (Stewart-Brown 1998). And on this view, it is not implausible to suppose that religious belief, by helping people to preserve their sense of the meaning and value of life, might contribute to the prevention of physical disease.

RELIGION AND THE PREVENTION OF MORBIDITY

Levin, as already noted, argues that the greatest accumulation of evidence for a positive connection between religion and well-being in later life turns on the prevention of physical morbidity. If this point is accepted, there is a good case for saying that, in the present state of knowledge, the practical implications of these findings for health policy are very limited. On this reading of the evidence, the findings will have policy implications to the extent that they bear on the way in which the individual and the community exercise the ability to modify factors which increase or decrease the risk of ill-health. We should ask therefore what difference the findings make to the way in which we individually and collectively exercise our ability to modify risk factors for ill-health.

Research findings on the prevention of morbidity are often closely examined with a view to extracting their implications for individual lifestyle – for the choices individuals make about their everyday habits, pleasures and pastimes. To treat religion as a similar kind of lifestyle choice, which may be guided by the desire to maximise health and well-being, is to put religion in a category where it does not belong. This, at least, is how it must appear to many people. There is something rather ludicrous (or at the very least paradoxical) in the suggestion that people might be advised to 'take up religion' because it is good for their health or will make them feel better, a point which was not lost on a journalist who penned an article on the topic.

> Great news for health freaks who rely on therapy and plastic surgery to sidestep death. Now they can swap their vitamins for an offertory gift which might tag on a few extra years. (*Times* 13 Aug 1998)

Behind the journalist's jibe there is a serious point. There is a great deal of difference between recommending a change in behaviour (like joining a health club) or even the adoption of strategies for improving social integration (like joining a social club) and recommending membership of a religious group with all that usually entails by way of intellectual and moral commitments. There is something rather odd even in attempting to draw out the implications of a positive connection between religion and the prevention of morbidity for the way in which we as individuals exercise our ability to modify risk factors for ill-health.

There is a further point. If the salutary effects of religious involvement in later life are mediated by the tendency of religious groups to discourage unhealthy lifestyles or provide strong social supports, it is also arguable, certainly on the first health behaviour hypothesis and possibly also on the second, that the findings would add nothing to the stock of received wisdom about the prevention of morbidity in later life. They would merely confirm the importance of known health risks and reinforce current recommendations. If religious people are healthier than non-religious people because they are less likely to be smokers, then the health message is 'give up smoking' not 'take up religion'.

Do the positive findings on the health benefits of religious involvement have *any* implications then for health policy or the practice of health care providers? Levin (1996), for one, argues that it is not yet possible to say anything very much about the implications of these findings for the way in which we collectively exercise our ability to modify risk factors for ill-health, for the simple reason that it is not understood how it is that religious involvement produces these effects. What is needed is more research to show how the causal pathways linking religious involvement with less morbidity might fit into an ideologically neutral strategy for successful ageing. On this view, the research should be seen as part and parcel of a larger inquiry into the prevention of illness and disability in later life. Anything which appears to protect against morbidity merits further investigation; religious involvement appears to protect against morbidity; therefore more research should be conducted in order to see how the effect is obtained. For the epidemiologist, what makes the research especially interesting is that it opens up a new avenue of inquiry on a protective factor which appears to operate differently from more established factors, like health behaviour or social environment or genetic predisposition.

RELIGION AND THE ABILITY TO COPE WITH ILL-HEALTH AND DISABILITY

Not everyone shares Levin's reading of the research findings, however. McFadden (1995), for example, presents a fairly extensive list of what in her view are the practical implications of the research on the connection between religion and health, among which she includes "the supportive role of religious faith for elders coping with physical and mental illness". And Krause (1997), in an editorial in the *Journal of Gerontology*, declares that "if religion really has a beneficial effect on health in late life, then the goal of research should ultimately be to inform intervention design", by which he means "interventions with explicitly religious content" (such as religious counselling).

Krause and McFadden, unlike Levin, think that the research on religion and ageing has implications for the development of *clinical* services for older people. They argue that religion makes a significant impact on health status in later life by helping people to cope with illness or disability. Health professionals who work with older people should therefore be asking themselves how they might better integrate religion into their care programmes. Koenig (1998) draws the same conclusions from what appears to be the first prospective study of the effects of religious beliefs and activities on remission from depression in medically ill older adults. If religion really does "facilitate coping" in older people with disabling health problems, religious interventions take on clinical significance as means of activating or supporting coping strategies in patients. The provision of religious support to hospital patients can make a contribution to the attainment of the same outcome as that which is sought by the multi-disciplinary health care team.

How should this particular conclusion be squared with Levin's judgement that the "therapeutic efficacy [of religion] as a specific strategy for curing disease [or aiding recovery?] seems implausible"? The point is that the scope of Koenig's claim is quite limited. It is not being stretched so far as to say that religion might somehow or other reverse or halt in its tracks an underlying physical pathology. What is being claimed is that religion might modify the impact of underlying pathology on the individual's *sense* of well-being. Koenig's study does not look at the association between intensity of religious belief and clinical outcome in a sample of patients selected because of the nature of their medical illness. He has selected a group of patients who have a diagnosis of depression *as well as* some non-psychiatric illness and looks at one outcome only – depression. The association of chronic or seriously disabling physical disease with depression is well documented in the medical literature, which is why Koenig's study is of interest: he is looking at an extreme, but not uncommon, manifestation of the failure to cope with illness and disability in later life. Still, it should be born in mind that very different results can be obtained by asking about the association between religion and clinical outcome in people admitted to hospital with serious and acute medical problems (irrespective of their levels of psychological distress). King et al (1999) found that what they call strong spiritual belief (a variable assessed without reference to religious activity) was an independent predictor of *poor* outcome in a sample of 197 patients admitted to acute care in a London hospital.

The practical implications of research findings on the "supportive role of religious faith for elders coping with physical and mental illness" are best understood in the context of the kind of individualised needs assessment that is meant to inform the planning of health care for older people. Koenig (1994) argues that such assessments should take account of what he calls spiritual concerns because there is evidence to suggest that religious support might have an important part to play in the health care of *some* older people, which is why he advises against "initiating religious interventions, as a matter of routine, before completing a full assessment of the patient's spiritual needs". The aim is to deliver the appropriate intervention to the right people. In this limited and specialised context the introduction of the idea of spiritual need should not be taken to imply that doctors or other health professionals should be responsible for the spiritual well-being of older people. The point is rather that doctors etc., in exercising their responsibilities for the health of older people, should take account of any factors that can be shown to contribute to the maintenance or recovery of health.

From one point of view this seems all rather innocuous and uncontroversial. It may be presented as a superfluous justification for what is anyway the *status quo*. Older people in hospital already have access to religious support, and there is surely nothing problematic in the proposal that people who *want* to see a chaplain or rabbi or any other religious specialist should be able to do so. Similarly "no-one can object to respectful support [from doctors] for patients who draw upon religious faith in times of illness" (Sloan et al 1999). Koenig, however, is making a stronger point. Once religious support comes to be seen as an adjunct to the therapeutic strategies of medicine, it is hard to avoid the conclusion that health professionals acquire some kind of responsibility for ensuring that it is deployed to good effect (i.e. to maximise health gain).

Koenig writes from the conviction that the resources of religion are under-used in health care. Or, to put it another way, that many older people who require health care are not making full and effective use of their personal spiritual resources. Because "religious faith has a supportive role for elders coping with physical and mental illness", providers of health care are urged to see to it that the health benefits of religion are more widely distributed among older people suffering from ill-health or disability. Behind this recommendation there is an assumption that there is a large fraction of the older population that might be helped to a more complete realisation of the benefits of their association with organised religion. The target group is comprised of those older people who stand to gain by strengthening an association which is relatively weak but not merely nominal. It appears to be one of the main purposes of what Koenig calls spiritual needs assessment to identify this group of people so that they may receive appropriate religious support. Such assessments enable the health professionals to ascertain what spiritual resources the patient might be able call on and so actively encourage their use. In a country like the USA, where such a large proportion of the older population affirm, in one way or another, the importance of their association with organised religion, the fraction who stand thus to gain might well be a significant proportion of the older population as a whole.

Krause (1997) recognises that there are "formidable ethical and practical challenges" in working out the implications of these arguments. This is undoubtedly true if we are to conclude that health care providers or health professionals should be *encouraging* or *promoting* the use of coping strategies that rely on the resources of organised religion. As Marwick (1995) asks, "should physicians prescribe prayer?" And yet the conclusion *seems* hard to resist once we start to talk about religious belief as a kind of personal resource which can be deployed alongside other therapeutic modalities in order to maximise health gain.

> Between the extremes of rejecting the idea that religion and faith can bring comfort to some people coping with illness and endorsing the view that physicians should actively promote religious activity among patients lies a vast uncharted territory in which guidelines for appropriate behaviour are needed urgently. (Sloan et al 1999)

RELIGION AND WELL-BEING IN LATER LIFE

If older people (in the USA) are asked about what 'keeps them going' during difficult circumstances, a substantial minority (20–30%) are likely to offer a religious response without any prompting of alternatives. If they are asked more directly about the helpfulness of religious beliefs in coping with life's difficulties, a substantial majority will answer affirmatively (Koenig 1993). Religious coping strategies may be relevant therefore to a wider range of problems than those that arise from ill-health and disability (Pargament 1997). Are they effective in these situations? Do they *really* help to maintain morale and facilitate adjustment? There are some quite large-scale studies (for example, Koenig 1988; Ellison 1991) which report a positive association between religion and morale in later life. There are others, however, designed to answer the same question and also fairly large scale, which can detect no association (for example, Steinitz 1980; Markides and Levin 1987).

McFadden, despite her reservations about the quality of the evidence for a causal relationship between religion and life satisfaction/subjective well-being/morale, concludes her 1995 review of the research findings of the salutary effects of religion in later life with a catalogue of their implications for policy and practice.

> Social services need to recognise that many older people turn to their churches first when challenged by health problems, economic difficulties and loss. Long-term care facilities need to assess whether they are meeting the spiritual needs of elderly people as well as physical, psychological and social needs.... Seminaries need to instruct future clergy about issues of aging and older adulthood.... Calls are emanating from the medical field regarding the supportive role of religious faith for elders coping with physical and mental illness.... Congregations should examine their programs and policies to see how elder-friendly they are. (McFadden 1995)

There is an air of comprehensiveness in this list; it is hard to think of anything that might have been omitted. Secular providers of health and social care to older people are urged to review their practices and policies on matters connected with religion and spiritual need, and religious organisations are urged to review their practices and policies insofar as they affect older people. Although it would be hard to gainsay either proposal, what is questionable is their relationship to the research findings on the benefits of religious involvement.

Quite apart from her doubts about the strength of the evidence, it is not clear why she should enlist research results on the salutary effects of religion in support of (some of) the points she wants to make. Is it not enough to recognise that, for many people, religion *matters*? Consider whether the *absence* of evidence for the salutary effects of religion in later life would justify neglect by congregations of their older members. Would a lack of evidence for the (psychological?) benefits of religion justify long-term care facilities or social services departments in going about their business as if religion did not matter to many of the people for whom they were providing care? Surely it is a mistake to suppose that evidence for the salutary effects of religion is required to make a case for changes in policy and practice on the part of either religious organisations or for example the providers of residential care, especially if it is acknowledged that the evidence is in many respects rather flimsy. It would be better to talk about duties and rights and justice. If churches are neglecting their older members, they should change because they owe it to the older members to treat them fairly and considerately. If providers of long-term care make no effort to help frail residents keep in touch with the religious community to which they belong, they should change because of the nature of the duty of care that they owe to these residents (see below).

The point of this scepticism is to press home the 'so what?' question. Let us accept (what seems anyway to be questionable) that researchers can point to positive effects from religious involvement on a dimension of personal well-being that is both measurable and independent of health status. From the point of view of the social and behavioural sciences this is really quite interesting. Certainly it is easy to see how the claim might attract much partisan comment. But what does it have to do with anyone's policy or practice?

ENGAGING WITH POLICY AND PRACTICE: SPIRITUAL OUTLOOKS AND SPIRITUAL BENEFITS

The empirical investigations that have been touched on in the previous sections by no means exhaust the interest of the connection between religion and successful ageing. It is perhaps no exaggeration to say that they barely scratch the surface. Much of the recent surge of interest in the topic has flowed into new channels of inquiry that have been opened up by a determination to reformulate the questions that have hitherto informed by far the greater part of the empirical research. The most visible aspect of this determination is the increasing use by gerontologists, as well as providers of health and social care, of the language of 'spirituality'. The intention is to redirect the research and reformulate the issues around the connection between *spirituality* and successful ageing.

There are two distinct lines of development to consider here. The first represents what is essentially a straightforward extension of the empirical research programme outlined in the previous sections. It argues that what Levin (1996) has called the social epidemiology of religion is defective in its account of religious involvement as a causal factor in the promotion of well-being in later life (Marcoen 1994). The outcomes of the research remain basically the same, however; the researchers work with more or less the same measures of individual well-being, for example, health status, self-esteem, etc. The second line of development is in many ways more radical. It asks for a reconsideration of the kinds of well-being that might be promoted by involvement in religion and has implications that go way beyond the attempt to redirect research religion and ageing.

The first line of development turns on the argument that individual participation in organised religion provides an inadequate focus for inquiry into the connection between religion and successful ageing. Empirical research which relies on measures of participation in institutional religion, even when supplemented by questions about the 'salience' of religion (see Chapter 2) in the life of the individual, concentrates attention on what appear to be the externalities of the religious life. To take the discussion beyond participation in institutional religion, researchers should ask about the contribution of a spiritual outlook to well-being in later life. They should ask about the way in which religion enables people to find meaning and value in their lives. It is here, after all, that we might expect to find whatever is *distinctive* in the contribution of religion to well-being in later life. Researchers should therefore endeavour to investigate the hypothesis that the operative factor in this connection is the cultivation of a spiritual outlook.

We need more knowledge about forms of successful and optimal ageing in which men and women may realise their full potential. How does a spiritual outlook on life relate to personal well-being and a sense of meaningfulness in old age? The study of the social and personal antecedents and the self-created living conditions of spiritually rooted well-being and meaning in life can lead to insights which are fruitful for the practice of psychological, spiritual and religious guidance of older people. (Marcoen 1994)

There are close affinities between this idea of a spiritual outlook and what is sometimes called intrinsic as opposed to extrinsic religiosity. Allport and Ross (1967), in what is now seen as a classic paper in the development of empirical measures of individual religiosity, propose for use a Religious Orientation Scale, which purports to distinguish people who "live their religion" from those who merely "use" it. To ask whether or not someone "lives their religion" is quite different from asking about adherence to articles of theological dogma or participation in religious ritual. It represents an attempt to assess the relationship between the beliefs and values of a religious tradition and the individual's most cherished desires and attachments.

One feature that serves to distinguish an intrinsic orientation to religion from a spiritual outlook is its relation to the beliefs and values of a particular religious tradition (Christian or non-Christian). Marcoen's proposed programme of research will appeal to anyone who thinks that there is a kind of common spiritual heritage shared by the major world religions, and will be even more attractive to those who regard the spiritual core of different religious traditions as more defensible than the claims that tend to separate different traditions (see for example, Küng 1987; Hick 1989). From this point of view it is possible, and even perhaps desirable, to dissociate the cultivation of a spiritual outlook from the ideas and practices of any particular religious tradition. And from here it seems only a short step to dissociate it from religion altogether.

The possibility of cultivating a spiritual outlook without any kind of religious commitment has considerable importance for the scope of the inquiry into the connection between religion and successful ageing. Instead of looking for characteristics that distinguish people 'with' religion from those 'without' religion, researchers would look for something like spiritual beliefs or a spiritual outlook that may be shared by either. It goes without saying that for the idea to be useful for the purposes of empirical research, there have to be people who *do not have* a spiritual outlook on life: the intention is to devise a distinction between spiritual and non-spiritual attitudes or beliefs. A clear example of what is at issue in this reformulation of the research question on religion and well-being is provided by King et al's (1999) study of the effect of spiritual beliefs on outcome from illness.

Religion pertains to the outward practice of a spiritual understanding and/or the framework for a system of beliefs, values, codes of conduct and rituals. It usually involves some form of communal religious observance. The term 'spiritual' usually refers more broadly to a person's belief in a power apart from their own existence. It is the sense of relationship or connection with a power or force in the universe that transcends the present context of reality. *It is more than a search for meaning or a sense of unity with others* [K Howse's italics].

Not everyone who is interested in the connection between religion and successful ageing welcomes the switch away from "religion in its teaching, organization and ritual". Levin (1996), perhaps the most tireless proponent of the epidemiology of religion, takes the view that the apparent advantages of the language of spirituality are spurious. It exceeds the warrant provided by any well-conducted empirical work and offers a recipe for confusion – better to stick with institutional religion. The idea of a spiritual outlook, with all its attendant problems of definition, is seen as a threat to the scientific credibility of a growing body of research which has only recently won recognition from mainstream funding bodies. Levin's criticism here seems somewhat harsh. The fact that some people might dispute for example King et al's definition is in a sense besides the point. It is for the research to show whether this particular construct is valid and useful in investigating differences in outcome from illness.

The argument that the notion of a spiritual outlook (or spiritual beliefs) is required to understand how it is that religion promotes well-being in later life has its complement in the argument that the idea of spiritual well-being is required to characterise the kind of improvement in well-being that might be effected by involvement in religion. Researchers should ask themselves whether it is possible to understand the contribution of religious involvement to well-being in later life without considering the possibility that it confers spiritual as well as non-spiritual benefits and whether (and how) it is possible to achieve these benefits without the mediation of religion. What is at issue here, and this is the second line of development in the use of the language of spirituality by gerontologists, is the adequacy of any description (or conceptualisation) of individual well-being in later life that does not make room for the dimension of 'spiritual well-being' (Moberg 1990).

Once again, the argument will almost certainly receive a sympathetic hearing from people who think that there is a kind of common spiritual heritage shared by the major world religions. It echoes, furthermore, precisely the kind of point about well-being that tends to be made in the religious literature on ageing. There is in fact a remarkable convergence between (some of) the religious and gerontological literature in their interest in the spiritual dimension of well-being in later life. Much of this interest can be traced back, as Kathleen Fischer intimated (see above), to the sense that it may be possible to age successfully even in the teeth of the kinds of decline and loss that are so common in later life, which means looking for a dimension of well-being or possible 'growth' that stands apart from those in which loss and decline are so often apparent. There is the sense also that there are "special demands made upon individuals by their own ageing" (see above), that there is a personal task associated with ageing – "how to accept it, appropriate it, give it meaning, and integrate it into oneself" (Curran 1981). What is distinctive and important in *this use* of the language of spirituality is that it is intended to highlight an aspect of the phenomenon of ageing which concerns everyone, irrespective of their religious convictions *or* their spiritual beliefs. This, for example, is what the Section on Spiritual well-being at the second White House Conference on Aging in 1971 has to say on the matter.

> In referring to man's spiritual well-being, we consider those aspects of life "pertaining to man's inner resources, especially his ultimate concern, the basic value around which all other values are focused, the central philosophy of life – whether religious, anti-religious, or non-religious – which guides a person's conduct, the supernatural and non-material dimensions of human nature".

This suggests, and this really is the burden of the argument, that the connection between religion and successful ageing has relevance for gerontology as a whole, because there is something in that connection which has relevance for all older people, and not only those 'with religion'. Not all older people are religious; nor do all of them have a spiritual outlook or spiritual beliefs. But *if* there is indeed a spiritual dimension to well-being, then they *all* have spiritual concerns or spiritual needs. This is the ground on which Barbara Payne (1990), for example, can argue that gerontologists who neglect the idea of spiritual well-being are closing off to view an important facet of the ageing process, something in other words, that promises to deepen our understanding of ageing. By the same token, policy makers who are concerned to promote well-being in later life should ask whether and how they should take cognisance of a spiritual dimension to well-being in later life.

What the language of spirituality offers to gerontological (i.e. non-religious or scientific) discussions of well-being in later life is therefore the possibility of overcoming the limitations of talk about participation in institutional or organised religion. The language of spirituality not only moves the discussion about religiousness in later life beyond the externalities of the religious life, but also it cuts across the boundaries that separate people from different religious traditions and those also that separate participants in institutional religious from non-participants. It affirms the possibility that people who neither have nor want to have any connection with institutional religion might cultivate a spiritual outlook, as well as the possibility that they might reap spiritual benefits from activities which have nothing to do with institutional religion. It requires us to stretch the policy implications of research findings on religious involvement and well-being in later life to take account of the position of people who neither have nor want to have any connection with institutional religion. If there are benefits associated with religious involvement in later life, is there no way of conferring these benefits on people who want nothing to do with organised religion? Is it not possible for older people who want nothing to do with organised religion to participate, and be encouraged to participate, in analogous, though non-religious, activities which have similar benefits? Is it not possible for non-religious older people to use coping strategies similar in operation and effect to those used by older people associated with organised religion?

RECONSIDERING WELL-BEING IN LATER LIFE: THE SPIRITUAL DIMENSION

There is little doubt that the language of spirituality, certainly within the Christian tradition, has taken on new life in recent years. Some of the impetus for the development comes from the desire to correct views of the religious life that place too much emphasis on conformity to prescribed belief and practice and not enough emphasis on the way that individuals incorporate religious goals and ideals into their 'inner lives'. The language of spirituality in this sense has a long-standing association with the idea of a way of life which is chosen with the intention of effecting a fundamental transformation of the individual; and in this context the idea of spirituality derives content and significance from the way it is used to explain the nature and value of such a transformation of the human person. The idea of spirituality marks off a particular aspect of personal life and confers a supremely high value upon it.

There is more to it than this, however. It has become common practice to use the language of spirituality as a kind of *lingua franca* for intercourse between different religious traditions – Christian and non-Christian. It is used to emphasise the importance of what different traditions have in common rather than what separates them. Christianity, Judaism, Islam, Hinduism and Buddhism boast large bodies of literature dedicated to the cultivation of attitudes of mind and practices that are intended to effect a fundamental reorientation of human desire and which derive their value from something more than their contribution to human well-being. It is hardly surprising therefore that the language of spirituality should also be the natural vehicle of a fairly widespread eclecticism in religious matters (Luckmann's 'invisible religion' – see Chapter 2). Nor that it should be possible to talk about, for example, the cultivation of a spiritual outlook in people without any kind of religious commitment.

One of the points at which the language of spirituality enters into the literature on ageing has already been mentioned earlier in this report. Representatives of particular religious traditions may ask whether or not there is anything distinctive about older people which might have implications for the way the institutions of the tradition exercise their responsibilities for meeting spiritual need or fostering the spiritual life. Do older people, by virtue of being at a different stage on life's journey, need a different kind of spiritual care or support from younger people? Are the spiritual needs (or goals) of later life different from those of earlier years? Are the conditions of spiritual well-being different? What should be done to meet the spiritual needs (or promote the spiritual well-being) of special groups such as older people in residential care or those with dementia? These questions, when asked by representatives of particular religious traditions, can be understood as part of various attempts to define the responsibilities of religious organisations as providers of spiritual care to older people and to consider ways in which they may evaluate their own work in this respect – their ministry. Theologians will want to decide whether these questions require of them a distinct theology of ageing or whether they can be answered in terms of moral categories like justice and equality (Webber 1984; Richard 1982).

The literature on the spirituality of ageing which can be placed in this way is in one sense quite straightforward. It is trying to answer questions about later life from the point of view of a particular religious tradition, and the basic outline of the answer comes from within the tradition. In other words, the legitimacy of the answer depends at least in part upon the content of the tradition itself. To ask whether these answers are right or wrong without reference to the tradition is to misunderstand the nature of the question: the authors are engaged in the exposition of a religious tradition, they are not scientists investigating an aspect of the psychology of later life. A very clear example of this approach to the matter may be found in the work of Gerard Hughes (1998), who is a Jesuit and believes that the tradition of Ignatian spirituality has all that he requires to answer the question: what are the spiritual needs (or spiritual goals) of later life? There are other books which combine the framework of a particular tradition with the ideas and techniques of counselling (for example, Sullender and Scott 1989; Guenther 1996). To say that this literature is firmly based within a particular religious tradition does not entail, however, that it has nothing whatsoever to say to people who reject the tradition. It may, like the work of Lyon (1985) and Bianchi (1982), set out to engage people who stand outside the tradition in a debate about well-being or fulfilment in later life .

Not all of the literature which combines an interest in ageing with the language of spirituality is so straightforward, however, and much of what has been written about dementia and spiritual well-being falls within this not-very-straightforward category. Although it stands within a particular tradition (almost invariably Christian), it can be seen to present a challenge to the tradition which is not merely practical but also conceptual (Petzsch 1984; Froggatt and Shamy 1995). If the churches are to take seriously their responsibilities for fostering the spiritual life of their older members, they must ask what this means for people with dementia. Are people with dementia to be excluded from the benefits of pastoral (=spiritual) care? And if they are not to be excluded, it is arguable that the providers of pastoral care should formulate an account of its specifically spiritual benefits of pastoral care which is applicable to them (Bruce 1998).

As this chapter has already made clear, the language of spirituality is not confined to discussions of ageing that are embedded more or less firmly in a religious standpoint. Questions are asked, in other words, about spiritual needs in later life (or the conditions of spiritual well-being or the nature of spiritual care or the benefits of spiritual maturity) in the expectation that the answers will be found elsewhere than in the ideas of a particular religious tradition. The difference is surely important. Insofar as the institutions of organised religion define their functions so as to include some kind of responsibility for guiding the spiritual life of their members, it is necessary for them to ask and answer these questions. When, however, questions about the spiritual needs or goals of later life become detached from inquiries grounded in particular religious traditions, we want to know *why* they are being asked and *how* they are to be answered. What is the rationale for asking these questions outside the context of an account of the responsibilities of institutional religion? And how are they to be answered other than by an appeal to religious tradition?

The pressures to adopt this use of the language of spirituality can be seen in two policy questions that might be asked about religious and secular providers of care to older people. What, if any, responsibilities do religious providers of health and social care have for promoting the spiritual well-being of older people in their care who are, so to speak, non-believers? What, if any, responsibilities do secular providers of health and social care have for promoting the spiritual well-being of older people in their care?

If a religious organisation thinks that its responsibilities towards the spiritual well-being of non-members are fulfilled through evangelism, there is for that organisation nothing more to be said. They have no interest in adapting their views on the spiritual needs and goals of later life so as to make them acceptable to non-members. If, on the other hand, they are an organisation like, for example, Methodist Homes for the Aged, which is responsible for the provision of residential care to increasing numbers of non-Methodists and even non-Christians, there is a great deal more to be said. The organisation is bound to define its responsibilities in such a way as to include spiritual care (or the promotion of spiritual well-being) and is therefore bound to consider how this responsibility should be exercised with non-Methodists. How closely should the exercise of this responsibility be tied to a particular religious tradition?

There are similar pressures prompting similar questions to be asked about the responsibilities of secular providers of health and social care. In this case, however, the questions are asked from a very different point of view. Secular providers of health and social care do not, as a rule, include the provision of spiritual care or the promotion of spiritual well-being among their responsibilities to the older people in their care. They tend to regard these matters as the province of organised religion and concern themselves solely with issues of access.

The first set of questions, those dealing with the responsibilities of the institutions of organised religion, can be left to theologians of pastoral care. Of more interest to us here are the questions about secular providers. Apart from psychiatry (Koenig's specialty), the main contexts in which these questions have been raised are: general nursing, terminal or palliative care and residential care.

MEETING NEED AND PROMOTING WELL-BEING: NURSING

The health care profession which has done most to stir up debate on spiritual needs (and their correlative spiritual care) is nursing. Much of the nursing literature on this topic looks to dissociate spiritual needs and spiritual care from institutional religion. It leads up to the view that the provision of spiritual care is the responsibility of the health and social care professions as well as chaplains and other official representatives of institutional religion; and as a corollary of this calls for the development of an expertise that helps with spiritual needs while being detached from any particular religious commitment or standpoint.

Many discussions of spiritual care in nursing are explicit on this point. For example, Dyson (1997), after asserting that nurses "need a working framework for the exploration of spirituality" goes on to argue that

> Although nursing as a profession strives to care for the whole person, in reality the physical, social and psychological aspects are stressed whilst spiritual care is ignored or left to chaplains or other spiritual leaders. The nursing profession needs to recognise its responsibilities, work closely with the multi-disciplinary team and identify appropriate assessment frameworks for spiritual needs, so that interventions to meet those needs can be planned and implemented.

Ross (1995), having surveyed various "definitions of nursing, codes of conduct, models of nursing and guidelines for nursing education", concludes that "spiritual care is a nursing responsibility, not an optional extra". Oldnall (1996) is also clear that nurses should not leave spiritual needs to "chaplains or religious representatives". What lies behind these various claims for an extension of nursing responsibilities is a certain view of holistic nursing practice.

> Patients have become customers and staff have become human resources. The therapeutic bond that develops between patient and carer [i.e. nurse] when truly holistic care is delivered has been weakened. Spiritual care is the missing element, and carers must learn how to deal with the spirituality of their patients and themselves. (Johnson 1998)

When illness is serious or life-threatening, holistic or whole person care is a *sine qua non* of the route to the recovery of health.

> While it is important to respond clinically to the illness, the [patient] will not achieve full health unless he or she is cared for as a whole person and the true impact of the illness explored in both personal terms and in relation to the individual's connectedness with others. (Speck 1998)

Granted that the nursing profession should be providing 'truly holistic care' and granted also that human beings have needs which cannot be subsumed under the catch-all tag of 'biopsychosocial' need, it is a very short step to the conclusion that nurses should be providing spiritual care. Berggren-Thomas and Griggs (1995) are in no doubt that "spiritual care is part of the basic holistic care that nurses provide" and go so far as to say that nurses should learn to see themselves "as persons who can enhance the spiritual growth of their clients".

The argument, cast as it is here in rather abstract terms, should perhaps be considered in the light of what seems to be the only British study of the spiritual needs of elderly hospital patients (Ross 1997). The conclusions drawn from this rather small empirical study could be fairly described as modest rather than ambitious.

> Some elderly patients interviewed experienced spiritual needs while in hospital.... Ways in which the elderly might be helped to meet their spiritual needs include enabling them to attend hospital services or providing a quiet room for prayer/reflection as well as improving links with the chaplaincy service.

These conclusions, similar in fact to those of Koenig (see above), fall short of the claim that provision for spiritual needs should not be left to chaplains and their like. On one view (the more modest view) nursing responsibility for the spiritual needs of patients would extend no further than the performance of spiritual needs assessments. In other words, health needs assessments would be modified to include, say, questions about religion and the importance attached to it by the patient. Responsibility for meeting needs would lie elsewhere than with the nursing profession. The more radical view would dissent from this on the basis of fairly general considerations to do with what is needful for human well-being, rather than the empirical evidence on the "supportive role of religious faith for elders coping with physical and mental illness".

Whether or not we recognise the claim of the nursing profession to be providers of spiritual care, the proponents of this view do highlight an issue of obvious importance. If one of the functions of the institutions of organised religion is to help foster the spiritual life of their members, and if it can be shown that the performance of this function provides these same members with spiritual resources which make a difference to their ability to cope with ill-health, what should be done about people who stand quite firmly outside the institutions of organised religion? Do they have a spiritual life which may be fostered or neglected? Is it possible to provide them with some kind of assistance in the development of their own spiritual resources? Who should be doing this and what is it that they should be doing? Clearly the key step in this line of reasoning is the assertion that everyone has spiritual concerns or needs. Empirical evidence for the health benefits of religion is of less relevance than the view that "the need for spiritual integrity is a basic human need" (cited by Ross 1995). Oldnall (1996) also invokes the principle that "each individual has spiritual needs regardless of whether the individual is religious or not".

As a result the focus of interest is shifted away from the non-spiritual benefits associated with the availability of religious support, and towards the idea of specifically spiritual benefits which may be shared by people who want nothing to do with religion. The efficacy of spiritual resources, or spiritual care, in people's lives is to be explained, not in terms of their supposed health benefits, but in terms of a basic human need, an aspect of our common human nature. And once it is accepted that it is both possible and desirable to help people to foster spiritual resources in themselves without in any way calling on institutional religion, we are faced with the challenge of devising techniques for fostering spiritual resources in people who neither have nor desire contact with institutional religion.

MEETING NEED AND PROMOTING WELL-BEING: PALLIATIVE CARE

It is instructive to compare the case of general nursing with that of palliative care. Palliative care, unlike nursing, is defined not by the professional competencies and responsibilities of the providers of care but by the condition of the recipients of care. Just as the nursing profession has more to say on spiritual needs and care than any other health or social care profession (largely because of its commitment to so-called holistic care), so do writers on palliative or terminal care and the hospice movement have more to say on this issue than those who deal with other clearly defined care groups (Twycross 1996). Palliative care has, of course, its own distinctive point of view on the issue of spiritual care, a point of view conditioned by the fact that death is for most people and self-evidently a time of momentous crisis. The specialty, which came into existence because of the perceived inadequacies of the health care provided to people who were dying from incurable disease, is committed to using medical and nursing skills to help people to 'a good death'. It also recognises that there is more to the care of the dying than the management of physical pain and discomfort. This 'more', which has to do with the way in which the dying person faces up to death, may be provided within a broadly religious framework (Saunders 1981) or within the framework of what might be called humanistic psychology (Kubler-Ross 1969). That providers of health care have a responsibility to make this 'something more' available to people who are terminally ill irrespective of their religious allegiance is a fundamental premise of the hospice movement. It has been argued also that the responsibility extends beyond the health care professions to social work (Lloyd 1997). It embraces all the many professions or disciplines that might collaborate in the care of the dying.

One of the connections between discussions of spiritual needs in palliative care and spiritual needs in the care of older people is obvious. Nowadays most deaths are deaths of older people. For the purposes of this report, however, it is more important to consider the implications of the analogy between care of the dying and care of the elderly. Palliative care provides a context in which talk about spiritual needs and spiritual care has a clear application. If it is reasonable to criticise the care that is given to people who are terminally ill not merely because of its failure to control pain and discomfort but also because of its failure to recognise that something more might be required, is it not also reasonable to criticise the care that is given to older people because of its failure to recognise the need for something more than orthodox medical and nursing care?

On the face of it, there are fairly important differences between care of the dying and care of the elderly. For one thing, there was a powerful and distinctive *moral* argument for changing the care of the dying. The argument was directed, firstly, against the failure of the medical profession "to regard the dying patient as a person rather than a collection of failing organs" (Callahan 1993), and, secondly, against dishonesty – individual, professional and social – in the matter of death. Is there a comparable imperative for change in the care of the elderly? It is also important to consider how we conceive of the 'something more' that is to be provided for in terminal care. The crisis of death is a crisis brought about by the knowledge of imminent personal extinction. The suggestion that the crisis may be rightfully avoided by suppressing the knowledge is now generally deplored. If palliative care does provide something more than orthodox medical and nursing care, it is to help people come to terms with the knowledge of their own imminent death. Is this a spiritual benefit conferred through spiritual care? If the help is provided by a minister of religion on ground prepared by the acceptance of a shared religious tradition, then there are few people who would quarrel with the description. If, on the other hand, the help is provided by a clinical psychologist to a patient who stands quite firmly outside any religious tradition, there are some who would resist the description of what is being offered as spiritual care and others who would insist that 'spiritual care' should be so defined as to include such a case. It is tempting to think that the only point at issue here is linguistic convenience. What matters is that we do not lose sight of the purpose of the something more to help people come to terms with the knowledge of their own imminent death.

What distinguishes the case of palliative care from that of ordinary health care of the elderly is that it is relatively easy to specify the nature and purpose of the something more than orthodox medical and nursing care that is provided in palliative care. It is more difficult to say what it is, apart from health gain, that we should not lose sight of when considering the benefits of the something more (than standard nursing activity) that is to be provided in non-palliative care. And it is similarly difficult to say what, apart from spiritual needs assessment, the content of this additional activity might be.

MEETING NEED AND PROMOTING WELL-BEING: RESIDENTIAL CARE

When the literature on general nursing or palliative care raises questions about spirituality, it rarely makes reference to the possibility that older people might have spiritual needs or concerns which are distinct from those of younger people. It is in the context of discussions about the kind of care that should be provided in residential settings that this particular angle on spirituality is most often explored. On the face of it, the analogy with palliative care looks much stronger than in the case of general nursing. In residential care settings, that is to say, the question about the something more that might be provided becomes more sharply focused.

Apart from those seemingly rare occasions, when the move into residential care is seen as a positive choice, it is often regarded as a momentous crisis, comparable in kind if not in magnitude with the crisis of death. There is considerable force in the metaphor which presents institutionalisation as a kind of dying to the social world in which the vast majority of people live out their lives. When institutionalisation is understood or experienced as an irreversible diminishment of life, a closure of opportunities and possibilities, a surrendering of the projects and pursuits which made life worthwhile, it presents the problem of the 'roleless role' in its most acute form. In these circumstances the something more to be provided would be a response to a loss of purposeful roles and projects. If we are willing to say that palliative care incorporates a spiritual component insofar as it helps people to come to terms with their own imminent death, why should we not say the same about residential care when it offers a considered response to the distress that might accompany a sense of loss of purpose and roles? By the same token, however, it is once again tempting to think that all that is at issue here is a matter of linguistic convenience. If some people wish to call this spiritual distress, so be it. (The labels matter only if they beguile and confuse us. We should, for example, be wary of talking about spiritual care as though there were a well-defined body of expertise and knowledge ready to hand for the alleviation of spiritual distress. The analogy with medicine is weak.)

Research studies which set out to describe the spiritual needs or spiritual concerns of older people in residential care are still fairly thin on the ground. What there is, is mostly American and much of this is grounded in attempts to evaluate or improve the kind of spiritual care offered by religious organisations to older people living in long-term care facilities. In the context of this kind of setting, it might seem appropriate to define the domain of inquiry (what aspect of human need are we talking about?) in the way suggested by the National Interfaith Coalition on Aging (NICA 1975). Spiritual needs are understood by reference to the idea of spiritual well-being, which is defined as "the affirmation of life in a relationship with God, self, community and environment that nurtures and celebrates wholeness". A paper by Lea Pardue (1991) on the 'spiritual needs of the frail elderly living in long-term facilities' provides an example of a study clearly set within the context of a concern for this particular aspect of the clergy's ministry to older people. The rationale for undertaking the study is that "nursing home residents have complex and profound spiritual needs which are frequently not recognised by the clergy serving them". The research exercise, conducted within the framework of the NICA definition of spiritual well-being, is to compare the views of residents and clergy on the best ways of meeting the spiritual needs of nursing home residents.

As soon, however, as the scope of the inquiry is widened to take in the (possible) spiritual needs of non-religious older people in residential care, it seems preferable to work with the sort of secular definition of spiritual well-being proposed by the 1971 White House Conference. In this case individual spiritual needs can only be understood by reference to "an individual's unique spirituality ... the way he or she seeks, finds or creates, uses, and expands personal meaning in the context of the entire universe" (Thibault et al 1991). It is with a statement from the 1971 White House Conference that Thibault and colleagues open their report of study to develop an "assessment instrument" for spiritual need in residential care. They share the view of the Conference that "all persons are spiritual, even if they have no use for religious institutions and practise no personal pieties". Their assessment instrument is for those "who want to help older adults to nurture the spiritual life by providing them with persons, things, and experiences which would maintain spiritual functioning and foster spiritual development and fulfilment". Their aim is more ambitious, more far-reaching in its implications, than the evaluation or improvement of the kind of spiritual care offered by religious organisations to older people living in long-term care facilities. "If the current cohort of elderly value spiritual activity, if it is a significant source of meaning in earlier life and continues to be so in later life, should not we make every attempt to nurture this source of meaning?"

Both Pardue and Thibault are American. Their studies are small, even slight, and may not perhaps qualify as examples of the kind of "thorough and extensive research" which Seeber (1990) wants to see conducted around this topic. The *Journal of Religious Gerontology*, which publishes most of the papers on this topic, is also American. In the United Kingdom the topic is only beginning to attract interest, though there is no doubt that it *is* attracting interest.

One recent British contribution looking specifically at residential care is Reagan and Smith's (1997) report on *The fullness of time*. What is notable about this publication is that it holds the language of spirituality at arms' length. The authors are well aware that the link between spiritual need or well-being and institutional religion has been much criticised, but they are reluctant to take up the challenge of formulating an alternative view of spiritual matters. The practical implications of their discussion for residential care may be presented therefore in the form of two options. Insofar as spiritual needs are understood in terms of the link with institutional religion, there are issues around poor accessibility (to spiritual care/support of the kind provided by institutional religion) and there are issues to do with even-handedness (of the sort that are bound to arise in a multi-cultural society). If it is insisted that the conceptual link between spiritual needs and religion is broken, they would rather dispense with the language of spirituality altogether, preferring to talk about the best kind of person-centred care. The scepticism of Reagan and Smith stands in marked contrast with the enthusiastic advocacy of a non-religious approach to spiritual well-being shown by Errollyn Bruce in her discussion of the possibilities of measuring spiritual well-being in older people with dementia (1998).

If we are to get to grips with the issues raised by these various studies, it is essential, in the first instance, to distinguish between the two kinds of residential care settings in which they might be raised. On the one hand, there is residential care provided by religious organisations which will tend to see themselves as having some sort of responsibility for the spiritual life of their residents. For these providers the question *whether* they should make provision for spiritual need does not really arise. They make this provision because of their religious ties. It is part of their *raison d'être*. And on the other hand, there is residential care provided by secular agencies. Secular providers of residential care are in a different position. For them it *is* important to consider whether or not their duty of care should be so defined as to include provision for the spiritual needs of their residents. Are *they* also bound to recognise that there is a spiritual dimension to the well-being of their residents?

In care settings with strong religious ties, it is likely that spiritual care will be woven into the very fabric of provision, which is after all the source of their appeal to older people with religious leanings. In these circumstances there are two kinds of policy issue which may confront providers. There are questions which turn on the position of older people who do not belong to the religious community with which the home is connected. Should they, for example, accept applications for residence from non-believers? And if they do admit non-believers, should they make separate provision for their spiritual needs? The providers might also, as in the US studies already cited, want to ask about the *quality* of spiritual care they offer, how they might improve the provision they make for the spiritual needs of their residents.

So what should religious providers of residential care do about outsiders, non-believers? It is not difficult to imagine a situation in which access to *any* residential care was tied to some sort of religious test; and it is clear that any such arrangement would infringe basic religious freedoms, which include of course the freedom *not* to participate in any form of religious activity. The situation would be parallel to that in which all residential care homes were rigidly secular to the point of excluding any form of communal worship. In the circumstances which now obtain in the United Kingdom, where there is a mixture of religious and non-religious provision, this particular problem does not arise, however. What matters is that providers are free to offer different kinds of provision – religious or non-religious – and that older people are able to choose from among them. A religiously exclusive residential care home infringes the basic religious freedoms of non-believers no more than the absence of religiously exclusive care infringes the basic religious freedoms of believers. What is at stake here are preferences rather than rights. There is, in other words, a good case based on preference satisfaction for trying to maintain a wide range of religious and non-religious provision. It is surely desirable that older people should be able to choose to live in care homes which number among their residents a large proportion of like-minded (or like-cultured) people. If religious providers are reluctant to close their doors to non-believers (and many of them are), they have a problem therefore, namely to decide by how much they can dilute the character of a home which makes it an object of preference for some older people.

Although religious providers do not have to ask themselves whether they have a duty to provide for the spiritual needs of their residents, secular providers *should* ask themselves this very question. It is important for them to decide, for example, whether they should provide their dependent residents with assistance in maintaining contact with their particular religious community. And should they take a similarly extended view of what they owe to non-believers, that is to say residents who belong to no religious community and have no wish to belong? In other words, should they understand this duty of care in such a way that it confers benefits on non-believers as well as believers?

If we insist, as seems right, that providers should actively help religiously inclined residents to maintain their religious practice, there are various lines of reasoning to which we might appeal in support of this view. The arguments are important because they provide a possible rationale for talking about the responsibilities of secular providers for the spiritual welfare of their residents. (It is interesting to consider how the position of older people in residential care differs in this respect from that of children in the eyes of the law. Providers of residential care are required by law "to ensure that every resident *under the age of 18 years* has so far as practicable in the circumstances the opportunity to attend such religious services and to receive such instruction as may be appropriate to the religious persuasion to which the resident belongs" [Registered Homes Act 1984].) Not all of them, however, are equally robust. It seems undesirable, for instance, to appeal to basic religious freedoms. What is at issue is not the freedom to practise a religion without fear of sanctions (sometimes called a negative right) but the right to *receive assistance* in maintaining a religious practice which may be threatened by disability and frailty (sometimes called a positive right). The right would be recognised not by *allowing* ministers of religion to have access to the home but by *ensuring*, for example, that a minister visits the home or that the resident is taken to communal worship.

It would be equally unsatisfactory to appeal to the non-spiritual benefits of religious involvement. Just as providers of health care are in the business of restoring or maintaining health, so providers of social care might say they are in the businessof promoting the well-being of their residents (though it has been argued that the aims of long-term residential care for older people are less clear-cut than those of health care, see for example Davies and Knapp 1981). In other words, there is a duty to promote the well-being of all residents and religious involvement promotes well-being (psychological well-being or life satisfaction), therefore providers should assist with maintaining religious involvement where appropriate. The trouble is that there is not much evidence that religious involvement does promote well-being (independently of health status).

A third option would be to approach the matter in terms of the language of 'needs'. What is important and distinctive about the language of needs in discussions of public policy is that needs are essential to human well-being in a way which creates duties (or confers rights). As there are different dimensions of human well-being, so there are different kinds of need to which all people are subject simply by virtue of being human. The providers of residential care should satisfy these needs in their residents because they are needs and not merely preferences. What kind of need is satisfied by receiving assistance in maintaining links with a religious community? It is part of the logic of the language of needs that they should be universal, in which case it seems better to postulate the existence of spiritual needs (which may or may not be satisfied by participation in organised religion) than to talk about *religious* needs. There is no sensible way of defining religious needs which would not restrict their application: a great many older people in this country will have no religious needs, no wish to maintain contact with organised religion. It can be seen, therefore, that *if* we adopt the language of needs as a basis for determining what providers of residential care should provide *and* insist that they have a duty to help residents maintain contact with organised religion, it is hard to resist the postulation of spiritual needs. And since, by definition, these needs are not peculiar to the religiously inclined residents, providers are faced with the task of determining what to do about the needs of non-believers. By this means we are enabled to say that the need to maintain contact with a religious community is the same kind of need that is met by trying to do something about the distress associated with a sense of loss of purpose.

There is another alternative, however, which is to argue that what is at issue has really nothing at all to do with religion. The right to receive assistance in doing something which matters to the person who wants to do it arises from the frailty and disability which creates dependence. If religious practice matters to older people who are dependent on the help of others to maintain their practice, then society owes it to them to see to that they are enabled to maintain the practice. To recognise this duty, it is unnecessary to have a view on why religion matters to some people or what the benefits (spiritual or otherwise) of practice might be. It is unnecessary to suppose that the practice is essential to well-being.

MEETING NEED AND PROMOTING WELL-BEING

The issue that the last few sections have tried to explore is the extent to which, or the ways in which, *secular* providers of health and social care should make it their business to provide spiritual care or promote spiritual well-being. That the institutions of organised religion (including religious providers of social care) are right to acknowledge such responsibilities is clear. It is not at all clear that the responsibilities of secular providers (including health professionals) should be defined so as to include provision for spiritual needs/the promotion of spiritual well-being. To accept this conclusion we should have to accept that the language of spirituality is somehow indispensable to our understanding of the aims of nursing care or palliative care or residential care. The implications are considerable. It will be necessary to investigate means of assessing and satisfying the spiritual needs of non-religious older people in health and residential care settings. Secular providers will have to sponsor the development of forms of care which promise to deliver spiritual benefits, only without the unwanted baggage of institutional religion.

SPIRITUALITY AND THE MEANING OF OLD AGE

Argument about the revision of the ideas about human need and well-being which inform and shape the provision of services for older people is by no means the only reason for gerontological interest in the spirituality of ageing. Barbara Payne (1990), for example, is interested first and foremost in "breakthroughs in the theory of aging".

> Reaching out to other disciplines, such as theology and the humanities, marks a breakthrough to move gerontologists beyond the primordial stage of our conceptualization of religiosity and spirituality toward an integrated approach to the aging process.

For Payne the idea of spirituality is important because it opens up new theoretical horizons for gerontology as a social science. It enables gerontology to progress beyond the two theories of ageing which have dominated academic debate since the 1960s – disengagement theory and activity theory. On the one hand, the disengagement of older individuals from social life was seen as beneficial to both individual and society. It had a useful social function. Activity theory, on the other hand, argued from the position that participation in meaningful social roles was needed to maintain a positive sense of self. On this view, which now dominates much of the social policy discussion of later life, the optimal strategy for ageing is to substitute new roles for those lost in middle age.

It is hardly necessary to spell out what it is that made disengagement theory seem unacceptable. It gave rational warrant to the rejection of older people by the rest of society. As they turned their faces to the wall, so could the rest of society turn its back on them. This is not to say that they would be denied the care they required. It is rather that they would no longer matter except as recipients of care. Activity theory also has its critics, however. Just as disengagement theory was evidently out of tune with emerging social trends, above all the emergence of the Third Age, so does activity theory seem to be out of tune with the realities of the Fourth Age. This, certainly, is how it seems to Thomas Cole (1986), one of the better known American historians of old age.

> The currently fashionable mythology of old age shows no more tolerance or respect for the intractable vicissitudes of aging than the old negative mythology. While health and self-control were previously seen as virtues reserved for the young and middle-aged, they are now demanded of the old as well. Unable to infuse decay, dependency

and death with moral and spiritual significance, our culture dreams of abolishing biological aging.

Daniel Callahan (1987) also, though for rather different reasons, is worried about what he calls the "modernization of aging" – a complex social project which aims to transform "the life of the aged from one of old-fashioned disengagement and preparation for death to a continuingly active involvement in life and a persistent struggle against decay and demise".

> There is nothing in that modernizing aspiration which promises to respond to the present root problem of aging, that of the need for a respected place for old age in society and in the lives of individuals. It may actually create new problems, at once offering no real alternative for the aged but to follow the crowd in their struggle against old age.... It is simply a prospectus for an individualistic old age as more of the same – more freedom and less responsibility, more years and less poor health – but with no illumination whatsoever about the meaning and significance of those years.

What Barbara Payne presents as a matter of scientific inquiry, Cole and Callahan present as a cultural malaise. They present the issue, not as one which belongs to gerontological theory, but as a matter of public concern, a proper object of public debate. For Cole ideas about ageing matter mainly because they shape the way that old age is experienced. They matter for Callahan mainly because of the way they shape the relations between generations. He fears that "an unlimited quest for individualistic pleasure on the part of the old" will undermine the strength of their claims to attention and respect, let alone help and support. It is for reasons such as these that "the interior meaning and contours of old age ought to be public issues, no less than debates about the indexing of social security payments or adequate housing" (Callahan 1987). The purpose of public debate in this case is not, of course, to influence the decision of a public agency, but to achieve a certain kind of shared understanding of ageing. What is wanted is, in effect, a shared sense of the values it is possible and desirable for human beings to realise in their later life.

How does this debate between critics and proponents of activity theory or the "modernization of aging" connect with discussions about spirituality in later life? The connection is made by McFadden when she says that

> With greater numbers of people reaching old age, the images of aging and well-being offered by religion will become increasingly important if they influence the social construction of late life as a time of possibilities for individual growth, service to others and individual fulfilment.

The connection with spirituality is also made more or less explicit by philosopher Harry Moody (1986) in the course of a discussion of the meaning of old age. Moody argues that there is no question but that modern society prizes activity to such an extent that the idea of what he calls contemplative receptivity has become almost unintelligible.

> This failure to understand contemplation poses a grave problem in the process of growing old today. Without some feeling for the virtues of ... inwardness, patience etc., it is impossible to understand what ego-transcendence in old age might ultimately be about.... We can only form a distorted image of it and call it quietism or disengagement.

It is easy to see that what is at issue here is nothing to do with the question of service provision, of doing something *for* older people to meet their needs or promote their well-being. In this context the idea of spirituality matters, not because of the way it shapes the provision of care in later life, but because of the way it shapes the *value* that is attached to a certain time or stage of life. There are two points to highlight in this discussion. The first is the contention that the "interior meaning and contours of old age" is a proper issue for public debate. The second is the way in which the idea of spirituality is set up in opposition to activity theory.

When Callahan says that the root problem of ageing is the need for a respected place for old age in society and in the lives of individuals, he is echoing a view that has been expressed by many of the authors and organisations cited in this study. He is echoing the views, for example, of the first White House Conference as well as those of the Board of Responsibility of the Church of England. What makes the views of Callahan and others of special interest is their insistence that it is not enough to replace a negative view of ageing with a positive view. They want to steer a path between a view of old age as a time when nothing is possible except endurance and nothing desirable other than the termination of suffering, and a view of later life as an open horizon which can be restricted only by defeatism or blinkered ideology. They want to deal with the issue of the public or social meaning of old age whilst avoiding the twin errors of bleak pessimism and naive optimism.

What is wrong with the negative view of ageing is that the significance and socially prescribed status of old age is determined solely by the position of dependency that is occupied by older people. There is nothing to raise old age *per se* in the estimation of the community, nothing to admire or desire except the ability to endure. What is of concern in the positive view of ageing is that it leaves the underlying problem unresolved. Although it rejects the position of social dependency, it fails to supply any *shared* view of the values that might be realised in later life. What we admire is the ability of some older people to postpone the onset of old age, to resist the losses that come with biological ageing.

The claim that it is necessary to have a shared view of the meaning of old age is based on the conviction that resistance may postpone the problem, but cannot eliminate it. It is true that at any one time most older people are independent and capable of being net contributors to the welfare of the community in socially recognised ways (for example, as grandparents or community volunteers). Eventually, however, most older people are deprived because of biological ageing of the ability to make these kinds of contribution to the welfare of the community. What we lack as a community is a shared sense of what is possible when the vigour of the Third Age is replaced by increasing dependence. Because we have no shared sense of the contribution that *this* stage of life makes to the life of the individual, there are no socially recognised ways in which people in this stage of life may contribute to the welfare of the community. Because we expect nothing of old age (hoping only for its postponement), we can expect nothing of people who are old. This essentially is what Callahan means by saying that old age has no respected place in society or in the lives of individuals. And it is why he thinks that the issue is one for public debate. Our society should try to recover or reconstruct a shared sense of the positive significance of that time of life we call old age – a shared sense of the nature of its contribution to human fulfilment. How else should this be done if not by public debate? This is not an academic problem to be solved by the theorising of experts: it is a political problem.

There is an obvious objection to these views put forward by Callahan and those who think like him. What he says runs counter to the prevailing philosophy of the age. Why insist on a *shared* sense of the social meaning of old age? Why should not people have their own *private* sense of the values to be realised in their old age? Is it not better that there should be a *plurality* of views rather than one monolithic norm prescribed for all? Who is to say which view of the place of old age in the individual's search for fulfilment is right? It is interesting that some of the religious writers on this topic show themselves to be acutely aware of the force of these questions, even though, with Callahan, they think it possible to provide satisfactory replies. Lyon (1985), for example, describes his purpose as that of "articulating an interpretation of human fulfilment in old age that can incorporate the wisdom of pluralism without thereby leading to the privatisation of the meaning of old age".

The role assigned to the idea of spirituality in this debate should be tolerably clear. It is in the idea of spirituality that we are to find our sense of what old age may contribute to the life of the individual and the welfare of the community. Not that this is Callahan's declared view, certainly not if it is thought to entail any kind of religious commitment. He is not saying, for example, that some version of theism is a necessary ingredient of that shared sense of the meaning of old age which he wants us to recover. Like Moody (1986) he prefers the speculations of psychodynamic theorists (see above) on the nature of the human life course to the writings of the theologians. What matters in this argument however is that theologians and psychodynamic theorists are seen to occupy common ground. There is convergence between (some) religious and (some) secular views of the significance of old age in the human life course, and on this basis may be built that shared sense of the meaning of old age which he thinks so necessary. Many people think that the language of spirituality is ideally suited to this purpose (though others would prefer to talk about wisdom). What enables it to play this role is the reference to an aspect of life which is independent of those capabilities which tend to decline in later life. It points to a category of powers and strengths which can flourish in spite of biological ageing and may only reach their full maturity in the context of biological ageing. To make sense of this idea, to explain what these powers and strengths might be, is the aim of several of the publications cited in this study. Their argument is that a view of human life which has no place for such a category will be unable to find anything to admire and desire in old age *per se*, though it will of course find plenty to admire in the lives of particular older people, especially those who remain active and keep busy.

CONCLUSION

If there is one conclusion to be drawn from the various arguments that have been propounded in this chapter, it is this. Once we turn our attention away from the responsibilities of religious organisations, the practical implications of what has been written about religion and spirituality in later life are uncertain and open to dispute. In the United Kingdom, where little empirical research has been conducted on religious involvement and spirituality in older people, it is easy to make a case for conducting more research. It would be interesting, for example, to see whether religious coping strategies are as widespread among older people in this country as they appear to be in the USA. It would be interesting to attempt to assess their effectiveness in residential care settings, and to see what came out of different kinds of approach to the assessment of spiritual need. However, what is needed as least as much as research is debate about the framework of ideas which would give this research meaning and significance outside the religious community. Above all, we should ask whether the language of spirituality is useful, let alone indispensable, for conducting debates and framing policies which are of great importance for the well-being of people in later life.

POLICY AND PRACTICE IMPLICATIONS

Does religion matter to older people in the UK?

That religion matters to a substantial minority of older people in Britain seems clear. Besides those whose religious allegiances are easy to identify, there is a group of uncertain size which would include older people who believe without belonging. These are people who have what King et al (1999) would call 'spiritual beliefs', but do not adhere to the practices or beliefs of any particular religious tradition.

That religion matters to a substantial minority of older people in the UK is a limited claim and, on the face of it, it would seem to have limited implications for the social policy of old age. Its implications for the institutions of organised religion are a different matter. If it is fair to say that some Christian churches have rather neglected their older members, and this is a criticism which comes mainly from the churches themselves, then they should consider how they might change their policies and practice to rectify this matter. They should ask themselves whether they do enough to acknowledge the contribution of older people (who probably do not think of themselves as old) to the life of the religious community. They should ask themselves whether they are doing enough for those older people who are at risk of losing touch with the religious community which matters to them. Finally they should ask themselves how, in fulfilling their responsibilities for nourishing the spiritual life of their members, by providing the kind of pastoral care which is their special sphere of competence, they might take account of what is distinctive in the position and circumstances of older people.

These are all questions of considerable importance and interest to churches and other religious organisations. It is arguable that such questions are matters of *public* policy only in the limited way that the affairs of any voluntary association are a matter of public policy: their actions become a matter of public concern only to the extent that they push up against the limits of what is socially permissible. If it is accepted that it is for the churches, within these limits, to determine the nature of their responsibilities towards older people in the light of their own organisational aims and values, secular agencies should tread carefully if they take it upon themselves to consider the ways in which religious organisations exercise their responsibilities. There is a big difference between making recommendations on matters of *public* policy and making recommendations about the policies and activities of a *private* (i.e. not public) agency.

Does the fact that religion matters to a substantial minority of older people in Britain have *no* implications then for the social policy of old age? No. It is something which providers of health and social care should take into account: they should not go about their business as if religion did not matter to the people to whom they are providing care. The implications are clearest perhaps in respect of the provision of any kind of long-term care to older people. The need for long-term care, in the form either of residential care or social care in the community, says something about a person's ability to maintain the way of life he or she followed before the need for care arose. If older people need help to do something which they set great store by, such as maintaining contact with a religious community or having a particular space for private devotions, providers of residential care should help them to do it. Providers of social care to older people living in their own homes should be asking themselves similar questions: whether there is anything they can do to help older people sustain a part of their life which disability and isolation might threaten to undermine.

All this is fairly uncontroversial. There are points, however, at which the connection between religion and ageing leads on to a consideration of more contentious questions. The last thirty years or so have seen the emergence of a substantial body of research, mostly American but some of it British, which has set out to investigate quite far-reaching claims about the association between religion and the process of ageing.

Do older people turn increasingly to religion in later life?

The interest of the claim that older people turn increasingly to religion in later life lies in the suggestion that "aging itself contributes to a deepening of religious concern in later life" (Moberg 1993). In other words, surveys which tell us that religion plays a larger part in the lives of older people than younger people also tell us something about the process of ageing; there is more to it than the fact that earlier generations – older people – are more likely than later generations – younger people – to have received a religious upbringing. To say simply that religion matters to some older people in this country is to underestimate its more general significance for our understanding of ageing.

What gives bite to the suggestion that we have to look beyond generational differences in religious socialisation to something that characterises ageing *per se* is the way it touches on the interests, not only of those who think that the lives of older people are too much hedged around with the pressures of social expectation and with myths about ageing, but also those whose concern with ageing runs alongside strongly held views on the place that religion *should* occupy in our lives. The former may well think that here surely is a generalisation about ageing that is just asking to be knocked on the head. As for the latter, consider, for example, someone like Richard Dawkins, the evolutionary biologist, who thinks of religious belief as a sign of weakness and folly; he would be understandably dismayed to hear that ageing *per se* made people more susceptible to weakness and folly. By the same token, to anyone who thinks that an increasing preoccupation with religion is *appropriate* to later life, it may seem fitting that ageing, as an ineradicable feature of the human condition, somehow draws people towards the same goals as those which religion urges them to pursue.

As it happens, the claim that "aging itself contributes to a deepening of religious concern in later life" rests largely on evidence from cross-sectional surveys which remains open to explanation in terms of generational differences. Attempts to find evidence (from longitudinal surveys and time-series data) which tip the scales firmly in favour of one interpretation or another also seem to be open to dispute. What then of the intrinsic plausibility of the claim? This surely must be closely tied to our understanding of the idea of deepening religious concern. It is not implausible to suppose that ageing should be accompanied by a deepening of faith in those who are already attached to a religious tradition, but only in a rather superficial way. It is less plausible to suppose that there are analogous changes of outlook in non-believers or people who believe without belonging, unless perhaps what is meant by the idea of "deepening religious concern" is simply an increasing concern with taking stock of life, an increasing preoccupation with the thought of death, wondering whether it all makes sense. On these questions also it has to be said that the survey evidence does not yet take us very far.

A great deal of the interest attracted by empirical research into the part played by religion in the lives of older people turns then on the claim that the results tell us something important about the phenomenon of human ageing. What is true of research into the *prominence* of religion in the lives of older people is also true of research into the *benefits* of religion in later. In this case, however, there is an added interest in the connection with public policy.

Does religion make a positive contribution to well-being in later life?
The claim that religion makes a positive contribution to well-being in later life because it helps people to adjust to or cope with the distressing and burdensome aspects of ageing undoubtedly goes beyond the available evidence on the association between religion and well-being in later life. At least it does so, if it intended to say more than that religion helps *some* older people cope with their burdens and difficulties.

The claim, whatever we think of the evidence on which it currently rests, would seem to imply that religion has a significant contribution to make to what are recognised goals of public policy. If religion does indeed help older people to adapt to the special and unprecedented demands of their changing situation (their ageing), then it performs, from the point of view of public policy, a useful function in the lives of older people. Does this mean that secular providers of health and social services should in some way co-opt religion in the pursuit of their aims? Have they something to learn from the way religion helps people to adjust to or cope with the distressing and burdensome aspects of ageing? Should they be considering ways and means of extending benefits which they recognise as desirable to people who want nothing to do with institutional religion? These are perhaps the most important of the issues raised by the growing body of research on the association between religion and well-being in later life.

A spiritual dimension to well-being in later life?

The claim that service providers and policy makers, as well as researchers, should expand their conception of well-being in later life to include a spiritual dimension is implicit in much of the work that has been reviewed in this report. What lies behind this claim, certainly as far as service providers are concerned, is not so much evidence as conviction and principle.

There is, for example, the conviction that secular providers really do have something to learn from the way in which religion helps people to adjust to or cope with the distressing and burdensome aspects of ageing: it *should* be possible to adapt religious coping strategies so that they are acceptable to people who want nothing to do with organised religion, people with and without religious beliefs. What lends colour to this view is a shift of interest away from the ordinary non-spiritual benefits associated with religious involvement, to consider specifically *spiritual* benefits which may be shared by people who want nothing to do with religion.

Closely allied to this there is the conviction that there is something of considerable importance that is missing from much of the health and social care that is offered to older people, and that this something may be usefully described in the language of spirituality. These two points are distinct. That is to say, it is possible to accept that there is something important missing from much of the health and social care offered to older people, and yet reject the suggestion that this something more is a response to *spiritual* distress or need.

That the institutions of organised religion may find the language of spirituality useful is indisputable. For secular providers of health and social care, however, it is certainly not indispensable. What would seem to be most important in all this is a firm grasp of whatever it is that is thought to be missing from much of the health and social care offered to older people. Arguments which proceed from what are surely questionable theories about the nature of human needs are an insecure basis for a critical review of provision.

"The goal is not to keep busy"

Arguments about the deficiencies of service provision for older people are not the only routes through which the language of spirituality enters into discussions of the social policy of ageing. It also connects with important questions that can be asked about our conception of the powers and capacities of the ageing human individual. What, for example, are we to make of the idea that the dignity of old age has its basis in the intrinsic worth and value of a time of life usually associated with a diminishing contribution to the welfare of the community? How are we to respect older people (and ourselves when we are old) not for what they have been but for what they *are*? What underlies both these questions (which are packed with presuppositions of various kinds and call out for further analysis) is concern over the idea of productive and active ageing. It is easy enough perhaps to see how these questions might be answered from within particular religious traditions but much less easy to see how they should be answered in a society without a common religious culture. The language of spirituality serves as a substitute for a common religious culture in some of the criticisms that have been levelled at ideas and images of ageing that play down the importance of the personal task associated with ageing – "how to accept it, appropriate it, give it meaning, and integrate it into oneself". This is an aspect of ageing which gerontologists have only recently started to investigate. The discussion of these issues, however, should not be confined to academic or religious circles – they are issues of public importance which merit wider debate.

REFERENCES

Abercrombie N et al (1970). Superstition and religion: the God of the Gaps. *Sociological Yearbook of Religion in Britain*. Vol 3.

Abrams M (1980). *Beyond three score and ten: a second report on a survey of the elderly*. London: Age Concern England.

Abrams M, Gerard D and Timms N (1985). *Values and social change in Britain*. Basingstoke: Macmillan.

Abrams P, Abrams S and Humphrey R (1981). *Action for care: a review of Good Neighbour Schemes in England*. London: Volunteer Centre.

Abrams P (1985). Policies to promote informal care: some reflections on voluntary action, neighbourhood involvement and neighbourhood care. *Ageing and Society*; 5: 1-18.

Age Concern England (1980). *Claim to be heard. The report of a working party set up by Age Concern England to study the role of religious organisations in the welfare of the elderly*. London: Age Concern England.

Ainsley SC and Smith RD (1984). Aging and religious participation. *Journal of Gerontology*; 39: 357-63.

Allport GW and Ross JM (1967). Personal religious orientation and prejudice. *Journal of Personality and Social Psychology*; 5: 432-43.

Amoss P and Harrell S (1981). *Other ways of growing old: anthropological perspectives*. Stanford: Stanford University Press.

Ballard P (1990). *Issues in church-related community work. A report for the British Council of Churches*. Cardiff: University College Wales.

Barker D, Halman L and Vloet A (1992). *The European Values Study 1981-1990: summary report*. Tilburg: Gordon Cook Foundation for European Values.

de Beauvoir S (1977). *Old age*. Harmondsworth: Penguin Books.

Beit-Hallahmi B and Argyle M (1997). *The psychology of religious behaviour, belief and experience*. London: Routledge.

Berggren-Thomas P and Griggs MJ (1995). Spirituality in aging: spiritual need or spiritual journey. *Journal of Gerontological Nursing*; 21(3): 5-10.

Beveridge W (1948). *Voluntary action: a report on the methods of social advance.* London: Allen Unwin.

Bianchi E (1982). *Aging as a spiritual journey.* New York: Crossroads.

Birmingham Council of Churches (1961). *Responsibility in the welfare state? A study of the relationships between the social services and the churces in a city suburb.* Birmingham Council of Churches.

Black EI and Read DB (1947). *Old people's welfare in Merseyside.* Liverpool: Liverpool University Press.

Blazer D and Palmore E (1976). Religion and aging in a longitudinal panel. *The Gerontologist*; 16: 82-5.

Boyle J (1987). *Survey of Wandsworth's over-75s.* London Borough of Wandsworth.

Brierley P (1991). *Christian England: what the 1989 English Church Census reveals.* London: MARC Europe.

Brenton M (1985). *The voluntary sector in British Social Services.* London: Longman.

British Council of Churches (1976). *Community work and the churches. A report of a working group of the British Council of Churches.* London: British Council of Churches.

Browning D (1973). *Generative man: psychoanalytic perspectives.* Philadelphia: Westminster Press.

Bruce E (1998). How can we measure spiritual well-being? *Journal of Dementia Care*; May/June: 16-17.

Buckle R (1971). Mormonism in Britain: a survey. *Sociological Yearbook of Religion in Britain.* Vol 4.

Bulmer M (1986). *Neighbours: the work of Philip Abrams.* Cambridge: Cambridge University Press.

Burton-Jones J (1990). *From generation to generation: towards a Christian understanding of the role and care of older people.* Jubilee Centre Research Paper No 9. Cambridge.

Byrd RC (1988). Positive therapeutic effects of intercessory prayer in a coronary care unit population. *Southern Medical Journal*; 81: 826-9.

Callahan D (1987). *Setting limits: medical goals in an aging society*. New York: Simon & Schuster.

Callahan D (1993). *The troubled dream of life: in search of a peaceful death*. New York: Simon & Schuster.

Calley M (1965). *God's people: West Indian Pentecostal sects in England*. London: Institute of Race Relations.

Carey G (1997). *Care and dignity in the next millenium: will older people have a prayer?* The 1997 Abbeyfield Lecture by the Archbishop of Canterbury. St Albans: Abbeyfield.

Chester County Council (1984). *The elderly in Chester: a survey of the over 65s in Chester District*. Chester.

Chester R and Smith J (1996). *Acts of faith: a study of older people and their places of worship*. London: Counsel & Care.

Church of England (1986). *Faith in the city. The report of the Archbishops' Commission on Urban Priority Areas*. London: Church House Publishing.

Church of England (1990). *Faith in the countryside. The report of the Archbishops' Commission on Rural Areas*. London: Church House Publishing.

Church of England, Central Board of Finance (1995). *Something to celebrate: valuing families in church and society*. London: Church House Publishing.

Church of England, Council of Social Responsibility of the Dioceses of Canterbury and Rochester (1992). *The Report of the Working Party on Ageing*. Canterbury.

Church of England General Synod (1990) *Ageing. A report of the Social Policy Committee of the Board for Social Responsibility*. London: Church House Publishing.

Clark D (1970). Local and cosmopolitan aspects of religious activity in a northern suburb. *Sociological Yearbook of Religion in Britain*. Vol 3.

Cobb M and Robshaw V (eds) (1998). *The spiritual challenge of health care*. Edinburgh: Churchill Livingstone.

Cole T (1986). The 'enlightened' view of aging: Victorian morality in a new key. In: *What does it mean to grow old? Reflections from the humanities*, edited by Thomas R Cole and Sally Gadow. Durham: Duke University Press.

Cole T (1992). *The journey of life: a cultural history of aging in America*. Cambridge: Cambridge University Press.

Coleman P (1990). Religion, ageing and adjustment: questions for research. *Generations*; no.13: 10-14.

Copeland JRM (1986). The well, the mentally ill, the old and the old old: a community survey of elderly persons in London. *Ageing and Society*; 6: 417-33.

Cox B (1987). *The health and lifestyle study: preliminary report of a nationwide survey of the physical and mental health attitudes and lifestyle of a sample of 9,003 British adults*. London: Health Promotion Research Trust.

Crossman R (1976). *The diaries of a cabinet minister, Richard Crossman*. London: Hamilton Cape.

Curran C (1981). Aging: a theological perspective. Reprinted in: *Aging and the human spirit*, edited by Carol LeFevre and Perry LeFevre. Chicago: Exploration Press.

Currie R (1977). *Churches and churchgoers: patterns of church growth in the British isles*. Oxford: Clarendon Press.

Cummings E and Henry W (1961). *Growing old: the process of disengagement*. New York: Basic Books.

Davie G (1994). *Religion in Britain since 1945: believing without belonging*. Oxford: Blackwell.

Davie G and Vincent J (1998). Religion and old age. *Ageing and Society*; 18: 101-10.

Davies B and Knapp M (1981). *Old people's homes and the production of welfare*. London: Routledge & Kegan Paul.

Davies D et al (1991). *Church and religion in rural England*. Edinburgh: T&T Clark.

Davis Smith J (1995). *Life-long commitment: a study of volunteering and residents' activity in Abbeyfield houses in the UK, Republic of Ireland and the Netherlands*. St Albans: Abbeyfield Society.

Davis Smith J (1998). *The 1997 National Survey of Volunteering.* London: National Centre for Volunteering.

Dyson J (1997). The meaning of spirituality: a literature review. *Journal of Advanced Nursing*; 26: 1183-88.

Dwyer JW, Clarke LL and Miller MK (1990). The effect of religious concentration and affiliation on county cancer mortality rates. *Journal of Health and Social Behaviour*; 31: 185-202.

Ellison C (1991). Religous involvement and subjective well-being. *Journal of Health and Social Behavior*; 32: 80-99.

Ellison C and George L (1994). Religious involvement, social ties and social support in a southeastern community. *Journal for the Scientific Study of Religion*; 33: 46-61.

Erikson E (1982). *The life cycle completed - a review.* New York: WW Norton.

Faith in Elderly People Project (1991). *Called to be old.* Bradford and Leeds Metropolitan Districts.

Fischer K (1985). *Winter grace: spirituality for the later years.* New York: Paulist Press.

Forster PG (1995). Residual religiosity in a Hull council estate. In: *Contemporary mainstream religion*, edited by PG Forster. Hull: University of Hull Press.

Frankl V (1959). *Man's search for meaning.* New York: Simon & Schuster.

Froggatt A and Shamy E (1995). *Dementia - a Christian perspective.* Derby: Christian Council on Ageing.

Gaine P (1978). Ageing and the spirit. In: *The social challenge of ageing*, edited by D Hobman. London: Croom Helm.

Gill R (1993). *The myth of the empty church.* London: SPCK.

Gorer G (1955). *Exploring English character.* London.

Greeley A (1992). Religion in Britain, Ireland, USA. In: *British social attitudes 9th report.* London: Social Community Planning Research.

Greenlees A and Adams J (1949). *Old people in Sheffield*. A survey carried out for the Sheffield Old People's Welfare Committee of the Sheffield Council of Social Service, Sheffield.

Guenther M (1996). *Toward holy ground: directions for the second half of life*. London: Darton, Longman & Todd.

Gunter B and Vinery R (1994). *Seeing is believing: religion and television in the 1990s*. London: John Libbey.

Hanson J (1964). *Report of an enquiry into the social circumstances of old people residing in 241 bungalows in an area of South Shields*. County Borough of South Shields.

Harris M (1995). Quiet care: welfare work and religious organisations. *Journal of Social Policy*; 24: 53-71.

Hay D and Heald G (1987). Religion is good for you. *New Society*; 17 April: 20-22.

Hay D (1990). *Religious experience today: studying the facts*. London: Mowbray.

Hick J (1989). *An interpretation of religion: human responses to the transcendent*. Basingstoke: Macmillan.

Hornsby-Smith M (1987). *Roman Catholics in England: studies in social structure*. Cambridge: Cambridge University Press.

Hornsby-Smith M (1989). *The changing parish: a study of parishes, priests and parishioners after Vatican II*. London: Routledge.

Hornsby-Smith M (1991). *Roman Catholic beliefs in England: customary Catholicism and transformations of religious authority*. Cambridge: Cambridge University Press.

House JS, Robbins C and Metzner HL (1982). The association of social relationships and activities with mortality: prospective evidence from the Tecumseh Community Health Study. *American Journal of Epidemiology*; 116: 123-40.

House J, Landis K and Umberson D (1988). Social relationships and health. *Science*; 241: 540-5.

Howard V (1987). *Report on Afro-Caribbean Christianity in Britain*. University of Leeds.

Hunsberger B (1985). Religion, aging, life satisfaction and perceived religiousness: a study of older persons. *Journal of Gerontology*; 40: 615-20.

Hughes G (1998). Is there a spirituality for the elderly? An Ignation approach. In: *Spirituality and ageing*, edited by Albert Jewell. London: Jessica Kingsley.

Hunt A (1978). *The elderly at home: a study of people aged sixty five and over living in the community in England in 1976.* London: HMSO.

Idler E (1987). Religious involvement and the health of the elderly: some hypotheses and an initial test. *Social Forces*; 66: 226-38.

Idler E (1994). *Cohesiveness and coherence: religion and the health of the elderly.* New York: Garland.

Idler E and Kasl S (1992). Religion, disability, depression and the timing of death. *American Journal of Sociology*; 97: 1052-79.

Irish Council of Churches (1989). *An ageing population: challenges and opportunities.* Belfast.

Jacobovits E (1981). An analysis of religous versus secularist trends in Anglo-Jewry, especially during the past fifteen years. In: *Jewish life in Britain 1962-1977*, edited by S Lipman and V Lipman. New York: KG Saur.

Jerrome D (1989). Age relations in an English church. *Sociological Review*; 81: 761-84.

Jerrome D (1992). *Good company: an anthropological study of old people in groups.* Edinburgh: Edinburgh University Press.

Jewell A (ed.) (1998). *Spirituality and ageing.* London: Jessica Kingsley.

Johnson A (1998). The notion of spiritual care in professional practice. In: Cobb and Robshaw, *The spiritual challenge of health care.*

Jowell R and Witherspoon S (1985). *British social attitudes. The 1985 report.* Aldershot: Gower.

Jowell R, Curtice J, Park A and Brook L (1997). *British social attitudes. The fourteenth report: the end of conservative values?* Aldershot: Dartmouth.

Jimack M (1983). *Jewish senior citizens in south London: a study of social and community needs.* London: Central Council for Jewish Social Services.

Jung CG (1933). *Modern man in search of a soul.* London: Routledge & Kegan Paul.

Kark JD, Shemi G, Friedlander Y et al (1996). Does religious observance promote health? Mortality in secular and religious kibbutzim in Israel. *American Journal of Public Health*; 86: 341-64.

King M, Speck P and Thomas A (1999). The effect of spiritual beliefs on outcome from illness. *Social Science and Medicine*; 48: 1291-9.

Knapp M, Koutsogeorgopoulou V and Davis Smith J (1995). *Who volunteers and why? The key factors which determine volunteering.* London: Volunteer Centre.

Koenig HG, Kvale JN and Ferrel C (1988). Religion and well-being in later life. *Gerontologist*; 28: 18-28.

Koenig HG (1993). Religion and aging. *Reviews in clinical gerontology*; 3: 195-203.

Koenig HG (1994). *Aging and God: spiritual pathways to mental health in midlife and later years.* New York: Haworth Pastoral Press.

Koenig HG (1998). Religiosity and remission of depression in medically ill older patients. *American Journal of Psychiatry*; 155: 536-42.

Kosmin B and Levy C (1978). *Jewish identity in an Anglo-Jewish community.* London: Board of Deputies of British Jews.

Krause N (1995). Religiosity and self-esteem among older adults. *Journal of Gerontology*; vol 50B: P236-P246.

Krause N (1997). Religion, aging and health: current status and future prospects. *Journal of Gerontology*; vol 52B: S291-S293.

Kubler-Ross E (1969). *On death and dying.* London: Tavistock Publications.

Küng H (1987). *Christianity and the world religions.* London: Collins.

Lenski G (1961). *The religious factor: a sociological theory of religion's impact on politics, economics and family life.* New York: Doubleday Anchor.

Levin J (1987). Is frequent religious attendance really conducive to better health? Towards an epidemiology of religion. *Social Science and Medicine*; 24: 589-600.

Levin J (1994). *Religion in aging and health: theoretical foundations and methodological frontiers.* London: Sage.

Levin J (1996). How religion influences morbidity and health. *Social Science and Medicine*; 43: 849-64.

Levin J (1997). Religious research in gerontology 1980-1994: a systematic review. *Journal of Religious Gerontology*; 10: 3-31.

Levin J and Vanderpool H (1989). Is religion therapeutically significant for blood pressure? *Social Science and Medicine*; 29: 69-78.

Lowe S (1969). *The churches' role in the care of the elderly*. Oxford.

Lloyd M (1997). Dying and bereavement: spirituality and social work in a market economy of welfare. *British Journal of Social Work*; 27: 175-90.

London School of Hygiene and Royal College of Nursing (RCN) (1962). *A survey of the role of the churches in the field of social welfare in Buckinghamshire*. Report of a study group of doctors and nurses.

Luckmann T (1967). *Invisible religion: the problem of religion in modern society*. New York: Macmillan.

Lyon KB (1985). *Toward a practical theology of aging*. Philadelphia: Fortress Press.

McFadden S (1995). Religion and wellbeing in aging persons in an aging society. *Journal of Social Issues*; 51: 161-75.

Maidstone and District Council of Churches (1965). *Maidstone: a closer look. A review of social services in a prosperous county town*.

Marcoen A (1994). Spirituality and personal wellbeing in old age. *Ageing and Society*; 14: 521-36.

Markides KS (1983). Aging, religiosity and adjustment: a longitudinal analysis. *Journal of Gerontology*; 38: 621-5.

Markides KS and Levin J (1987). Religion, aging and life satisfaction: an eight year, three wave longitudinal study. *The Gerontologist*; 27: 660-5.

Martin B (1968). Comments on some Gallup poll results. *Sociological Yearbook of Religion in Britain*. Vol 1.

Martin D (1967). *Sociology of English religion*. London: SCM Press.

Marwick C (1995). Should physicians prescribe prayer for health? Spiritual aspects of well-being considered. *Journal of the American Medical Association*; 273: 1561-2.

Mass Observation (1947). *Puzzled people: a study in popular attitudes to religion, ethics, progress and politics in a London borough.* London: Victor Gollancz.

Methodist Homes Association (1998). *Age awareness: understanding the spiritual needs of older people.* Derby: Methodist Homes Association in cooperation with the Christian Council on Ageing.

Michaelson M (1987). Domestic Hinduism in a Gujerati trading caste. In: *Hinduism in England,* edited by R Burghart. London: Tavistock.

Miller S, Schmool M and Lerman A (1996). *Social and political attitudes of British Jewry: some findings of the IJPR survey.* London: Institute for Jewish Policy Research.

Mindel CH and Vaughan CE (1978). A multidimensional approach to religiosity and disengagement. *The Journal of Gerontology*; 33: 103-8.

Moberg D (1965). Religiosity in old age. *Gerontologist*; 5: 78-87.

Moberg D (1990). Spiritual maturity and wholeness in the later years. In: Seeber 1990, pp. 5-24.

Moberg D (1993). Religion and ageing. In: *Ageing and later life,* edited by R Slater and J Johnson. Buckingham: Open University Press.

Modood T and Berthoud R (1996). *Ethnic minorities in Britain: diversity and disadvantage.* London: Policy Studies Institute.

Moody H (1986). The meaning of life and the meaning of old age. In: *What does it mean to grow old? Reflections from the humanities,* edited by Thomas R Cole and Sally Gadow. Durham: Duke University Press.

Morse CK and Wisocki PA (1987). Importance of religion to elderly adjustment. *Journal of Religion and Aging*; 4: 15-27.

Murphy C (1997). *Dementia care and the churches: involving people and premises.* Stirling: Dementia Services Development Centre.

National Council of Social Service (NCSS) (1954). *Over seventy. Report of an investigation into the social and economic circumstances of one hundred people of over seventy years of age.* London: NCSS.

National Council of Social Services Central Churches' Group (NCSS) (1968). *The caring community: Good Neighbour Schemes.* London: NCSS.

National Federation of Housing Associations (NFHA) (1995). *Voluntary housing: sixty years on.* London: NFHA.

National Initiative in Evangelism (1983). *Prospects for the eighties. From a census of the churches in 1979 undertaken by the National Initiative in Evangelism.* London: MARC Europe.

National Interfaith Coalition on Aging (NICA) (1975). *Spiritual well-being: a definition.* Athens, Georgia: NICA.

National Old People's Welfare Council (NOPNC) (1968). *The role of the churches in the care of the elderly.* London: NOPNC.

Neuberger J (1997). Soul-searching for an answer. *Guardian* 17 Sept 1997.

Oldnall A (1996). Critical analysis of nursing: meeting the spiritual needs of patients. *Journal of Advanced Nursing*; 25: 138-44.

Owen TF (1960) Chapel and community in Glan-Llyn Merioneth. In: *Welsh rural communities* edited by Elwyn Davies and Alwyn Rees. Cardiff: University of Wales Press.

Oxman TE, Freeman DH and Manheimer ED (1995). Lack of social participation and religious strength and comfort as risk factors for death after cardiac surgery on the elderly. *Psychosomatic medicine*; 57: 5-15.

Pardue L (1991). Models for ministry: the spiritual needs of the frail elderly living in long-term care facilities. *Journal of Religious Gerontology*; 8: 13-24.

Pargament KI (1997). *The psychology of religion and coping: theory, research, practice.* London: Guilford Press.

Payne B (1990). Research and theoretical approaches to spirituality and aging: past efforts and future direction. *Generations*; Fall issue: 11-14.

Petzsch H (1984). *Does he know how frightening he is in his strangeness? A study in attitudes to dementing people.* University of Edinburgh Department of Christian Ethics and Practical Theology Occasional Paper.

Princetown Religious Research Centre (PRRC)(1994). Importance of religion climbing again. *Emerging Trends*; 16: 1-4.

Qureshi H and Walker A (1989). *The caring relationship: elderly people and their families.* London: Macmillan.

Rabins PV (1990). Emotional adaptation over time in caregivers for chronically ill elderly people. *Age and Ageing*; 19: 185-90.

Regan D and Smith J (1997). *The fullness of time: how homes for older people can respond to their residents' needs for wholeness and a spiritual dimension to care.* London: Counsel and Care.

Reid WS (1978). A study of religious attitudes of the elderly. *Age and Ageing*; 7: 40-5.

Rex J and Moore R (1967). *Race, community and conflict: a study of Sparkbrook.* London: Institute Race Relations.

Richard L (1982). Toward a theology of aging. *Science et Esprit*; XXXIV; 269-87.

Richardson IM (1964). *Age and need: a study of older people in north-east Scotland.* London: E&S Livingstone.

Ross LA (1995). The spiritual dimension: its importance to patients' health. *International Journal of Nursing Studies*; 32: 457-68.

Ross LA (1997). Elderly patient's perceptions of their spiritual needs and care: a pilot study. *Journal of Advanced Nursing*; 26: 710-15.

Rowntree S (1947). *A report of a survey committee on the problems of ageing and the care of old people.* London: Oxford University Press and Nuffield Foundation.

Rowntree S and Lavers G (1951). *English life and leisure: a social study.* London: Longmans.

Rudd T (1958). *Growing old.* London: Catholic Truth Society.

Saunders C, Summers DH and Teller W (1981). *Hospice: the living idea.* London: Edward Arnold.

Seeber J (1990). Spiritual maturity in the later years. *Journal of Religious Gerontology*; 7 (1/2).

Slater R (1995). *The psychology of growing old: looking forward.* Buckingham: Open University Press.

Sloan RP, Bagiella E and Powell T (1999). Religion, spirituality and medicine. *Lancet*; 353: 664-7.

Speck P (1998). The meaning of spirituality in illness. In: Cobb and Robshaw, *The spiritual challenge of health care.*

Stark R and Glock C (1968). *American piety: the nature of religious commitment.* Berkeley: University of California.

Steinitz LY (1980). Religiosity, well-being and Weltanschauung among the elderly. *Journal for the Scientific Study of Religion*; 19: 60-7.

Stewart-Brown S (1998). Emotional well-being and its relation to health. *British Medical Journal*; 317: 1609-10.

Sullender, R Scott (1989). *Losses in later life: a new way of walking with God.* New York: Paulist Press.

Svennegig M (1988). *Godwatching: viewers, television and religion.* London: John Libbey.

Thibault JM, Ellor JW and Netting FE (1991). A conceptual framework for assessing the spiritual functioning and fulfilment of older adults in long-term care settings. *Journal of Religious Gerontology*; 7: 29-43.

Thompson P, Itzin C and Abendstern M (1990). *I don't feel old: the experience of later life.* Oxford: Oxford University Press.

Tournier P (1972). *Learning to grow old.* London: SCM Press.

Towler R (1985). *The need for certainty: a sociological study of conventional religion.* London: Routledge & Kegan Paul.

Townsend P (1957). *Family life of old people: an inquiry in East London.* London: HMSO.

Townsend P (1962). *The last refuge: a survey of residential institutions and homes for the aged in England and Wales.* London: Routledge & Kegan Paul.

Troyer H (1988). Review of cancer among four religious sects: evidence that lifestyles are distinctive sets of risk factors. *Social Science and Medicine*; 26: 1007-17.

Tunstall J (1966). *Old and alone: a sociological study of older people.* London: Routledge & Kegan Paul.

Twycross R (1996). *Introducing palliative care.* Oxford: Radcliffe Medical Press.

Wadsworth M and Freeman SR (1983). Generation differences in beliefs. *British Journal of Sociology*; 34: 416-37.

Wakeling JD (1979). Spiritual neglect of the elderly. *Concord*; 13:11-22.

Walker D (1994). *Homes for a multi-faith society - questions and choices for believers: a guide to what communities of faith can do.* York: Joseph Rowntree Foundation.

Ward CK (1961). *Priests and people: a sociological investigation of religion in Liverpool.* Liverpool: Liverpool University Press.

Webber A (1984). Spirituality and old age. *Ageing and Society*; 4: 345-9.

Wenger C (1993). The formation of social networks: self-help, mutual aid and old people in contemporary Britain. *Journal of Aging Studies*; 7: 25-40.

Williams R (1990). *A protestant legacy: attitudes to death and illness among older Aberdonians.* Oxford: Clarendon Press.

Williamson AP (1975). *Aspects of the quality of life of the elderly in Armagh: report of a survey.* Coleraine: New University of Ulster.

Wistow G, Knapp M, Hardy B and Forder J (1996). *Social care markets.* Buckingham: Open University Press.